Every Teacher Is a Reading Teacher

101 Ways to Incorporate Reading into Your Classroom

Grades 2–3

By
Angela Clum
and
Lori Taylor

Published by Instructional Fair
an imprint of

McGraw Hill **Children's Publishing**

Authors: Angela Clum and Lori Taylor

McGraw Hill Children's Publishing

Published by Instructional Fair
An imprint of McGraw-Hill Children's Publishing
Copyright © 2004 McGraw-Hill Children's Publishing

All Rights Reserved • Printed in the United States of America

Limited Reproduction Permission: Permission to duplicate these materials is limited to the person for whom they are purchased. Reproduction for an entire school or school district is unlawful and strictly prohibited.

Send all inquiries to:
McGraw-Hill Children's Publishing
3195 Wilson Drive NW
Grand Rapids, Michigan 49544

Every Teacher Is a Reading Teacher—grades 2–3
ISBN: 0-7424-2698-X

1 2 3 4 5 6 7 8 9 MAL 09 08 07 06 05 04

The *McGraw·Hill* Companies

Table of Contents

Introduction 4

Creating a Reading Environment 5

Reading Standards Correlation Chart 6

Ways to Incorporate Reading into the Content Areas

Math 7

Science and Technology 39

Social Studies 71

Language Arts 99

Physical Education, Art, and Music 122

Reading Award 128

Introduction

> "My students are at so many different levels."
>
> "Am I giving my students enough reading instruction to make them successful?"
>
> "There are so many standards to cover, I just don't have the time to fit everything into my lesson plans."
>
> "What reading skills and strategies are the best to use with my students?"

The questions and statements above may sound familiar to you. If you have heard or thought any of these things, this book can help!

Reading is a part of every school subject and of everyday life. So why should reading instruction be limited to distinct thirty-minute lessons in the language arts block? Reading can and should be seamlessly integrated with content-area instruction in every teacher's classroom.

In the middle elementary years, students are improving their reading skills and moving toward using reading to learn. As they progress through school, students will rely more and more on reading for learning. Therefore, it is essential that they have a strong foundation of reading skills and strategies to prepare them for learning in all content areas.

Reading instruction in the content areas serves two purposes—to teach reading skills and strategies, and to teach content. The 101 ideas in this book are designed to provide the essential tools teachers need to incorporate reading in all curriculum areas. Each activity includes innovative activities for content instruction, while introducing or reinforcing specific reading skills and strategies.

The activities are a combination of content-area topics and reading skills and strategies. Feel free to adapt the strategies or topics to meet the specific needs of your classroom and students. These creative ideas can be easily revised to correlate with your curriculum by changing some of the content-area topics. Even if topics are changed, the reading strategies or skills remain the same, and the value and benefit of these skills still reinforced.

Give students the tools they need to not only enjoy reading, but to also acquire valuable information in their roles as life-long learners!

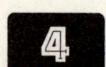

Creating a Reading Environment

The reading environment is essential to fostering successful readers. When building a positive reading environment, think of students' physical, emotional, and cognitive needs.

Physical Environment

- Make the reading environment inviting and comfortable. Create a reading corner with comfortable chairs, floor pillows, a rug, enticing lighting, and so on.

- Give students access to a variety of texts by providing books, magazines, newspapers, and Internet access. Read signs, ads, posters, menus, pamphlets, labels, boxes, and more!

- Provide regularly scheduled independent reading time in class. Encourage students to read at home. They can read to a younger sibling, or read anything of interest, such as comic books, children's and sports magazines, chapter books, and so on.

- Set a positive example. Make sure students see you reading along with them!

Emotional Environment

- Learn about students' reading habits, preferences, strengths, and weaknesses, and then provide books that address these issues.

- Help students create connections with text. Facilitate connections by activating prior knowledge, examining personal meaning, and respecting personal reflections.

- Give students the opportunity to choose titles to read. This gives them a sense of ownership, helping to engage them in the text and sustain interest.

- Create a safe environment for exploring and trying new things. Foster a feeling of mutual respect for reading abilities and preferences.

- Require that students read at an appropriate reading level. Text in any content area, including leisure reading, should not be too difficult.

- Get all students to participate in reading, no matter what their reading level. Try not to alienate slower readers. Give them time to finish before moving on or asking questions.

- Be enthusiastic about reading! Talk about books you love, and share your reading experiences and habits. Your attitudes about reading are contagious!

Cognitive Environment

- No matter the grade level, read aloud to students every day. Reading aloud provides many things: a good example, encouragement of creativity, language development, a love of reading, and much more!

- Help students build their vocabularies to make reading more successful. Create word walls, personal word lists, mini-dictionaries, and graphic organizers.

- Read for different purposes. Reading a novel requires different skills than reading an instruction manual. Teach students the strategies needed to comprehend these texts.

- Encourage students to talk about what and how they read. Use journal writing, literature circles, class discussions, conferences, conversations, workshops, seminars, and more.

- Writing and reading are inherently linked. Students can examine their own writing through reading and examine their reading skills by writing. Whenever possible, facilitate the link between reading and writing.

© McGraw-Hill Children's Publishing

0-7424-2698-X *Every Teacher Is a Reading Teacher: 101 Ways to Incorporate Reading into Your Classroom*

Correlation Chart

1. Read a wide range of texts.	7, 12, 17-18, 20-21, 23, 28-32, 37, 41, 43, 47-49, 51, 53, 55, 58, 60-61, 73-76, 78, 83, 89-90, 96-98, 106, 116, 120-121
2. Read a wide range of literature.	8, 15, 22-23, 25, 39, 40-41, 57, 60, 62, 64, 69, 71-73, 89, 99-104, 117, 122-125, 127
3. Apply a variety of strategies to comprehend and interpret texts.	7, 9, 16, 19, 25-26, 39, 41-46, 49, 51-54, 62, 64, 73-76, 78-85, 89-90, 96-97, 102-103, 105-108, 110, 113-114, 116, 118-119, 121
4. Use spoken, written, and visual languages to communicate effectively.	11-12, 14, 17, 20-22, 25, 34-35, 37, 39, 49, 53-54, 58-59, 71, 106, 111-112, 115
5. Use a variety of strategies while writing and use elements of the writing process to communicate.	12, 14, 17-20, 22-25, 43, 49-50, 62, 86, 111-112, 115, 120
6. Apply knowledge of language structure and conventions, media techniques, figurative language, and genre to create, critique, and discuss texts.	9, 12, 15-16, 19, 23-27, 41, 43-46, 55-56, 60, 64, 69, 78-80, 89-90, 96-98, 102, 108-110, 117
7. Research issues and interests, pose questions, and gather data to communicate discoveries.	10, 23, 34, 36, 38-39, 47-48, 55-58, 60-67, 73, 77, 87-88, 94-95, 122, 124, 126
8. Work with a variety of technological and other resources to collect information and to communicate knowledge.	10, 12, 23, 36, 43, 47-48, 55, 57, 60, 68-70
9. Understand and respect the differences in language use across cultures, regions, and social roles.	25, 78, 94
10. Students whose first language is not English use their first language to develop competencies in English and other content areas.	
11. Participate in a variety of literary communities.	11, 20-21, 23-25, 33, 39, 58, 66, 69, 118-119, 121
12. Use spoken, written, and visual language to accomplish purposes.	11-12, 21, 23, 28-32, 33-35, 37-38, 47-49, 55, 60, 73, 77, 88, 94-95, 99-100, 108-109, 111-112

MATH

1 Marvelous Math Stories

There are many wonderful books that have been written specifically for teaching math skills. Many titles are written in a story format, while others simply explore and explain a math concept. Create a special shelf, tub, or designated area in the classroom where math books are stored all together. Students can read these books when they have completed their math assignments for the day. The books can also be used as one of several rotating centers. Read stories aloud, so students can hear your reading voice. Reading quality literature aloud is an important modeling strategy for students. Also use big books with enlarged text so students can follow along with the words as you read. The illustrations are also large enough for all students to see, enabling them to look for picture clues as you read.

While reading, guide students to recognize how the author uses number words to enhance the visual descriptions in the story. Replace a number word from the story with one higher or lower to see if the same effect occurs or if different emotions are aroused. Numbers can be used to add intensity to any story!

Students also need to read aloud. Have students practice reading a math book several times. When they are fluent and can read it well enough to hold the attention of the audience, invite them to be the math story reader for the day. Students should read and reread text to develop fluency and expression.

After you read, invite students to answer questions to retell the story in their own words, stating the math skills used and then relating story elements such as character, setting, problem, and solution, as well as beginning, middle, and end. Students will develop their understanding of story structure while identifying how the characters use their math skills to solve real-life problems. Begin by doing this activity orally with the class after reading aloud a story. Post a list of math skills that can be used as choices to answer the question: "What was the math skill or skills used in the story?" Once students are familiar with answering these questions, have them write the answers in their math journals or on separate recording sheets. This activity can be done as a center as well. Students can present their retellings to the class as a book talk and explain why others should read the book. Consult the "Suggested Titles for Math" on page 8 for a listing of age-appropriate literature related to math.

Suggested Titles for Math

The age ranges and levels of these books vary. Use them according to students' needs, interests, and abilities.

Alexander, Who Used to Be Rich Last Sunday by Judith Viorst
Animals on Board by Stuart J. Murphy
Annie's Pet by Barbara Brenner
The Best Vacation Ever by Stuart J. Murphy
Betcha! Estimating by Stuart J. Murphy
Cats Add Up! by Dianne Ochiltree
Counting on Frank by Rod Clement
Divide and Ride by Stuart J. Murphy
A Dollar for Penny by Julie Glass
A Dozen Dizzy Dogs by William H. Hooks
Elevator Magic by Stuart J. Murphy
A Fair Bear Share by Stuart J. Murphy
The Fly on the Ceiling: A Math Myth by Julie Glass
Get Up and Go! by Stuart J. Murphy
Give Me Half! by Stuart J. Murphy
The Greedy Triangle by Marilyn Burns
The Gummy Candy Counting Book by Amy and Richard Hutchings
The Hershey's Kisses Subtraction Book by Jerry Pallotta
Hershey's Milk Chocolate Weights and Measures by Jerry Pallotta
Just Enough Carrots by Stuart J. Murphy
Lemonade for Sale by Stuart J. Murphy
The Penny Pot by Stuart J. Murphy
Ready, Set, Hop! by Stuart J. Murphy
A Remainder of One by Elinor J. Pinczes
Sea Squares by Joy N. Hulme
Spunky Monkeys on Parade by Stuart J. Murphy
Stay in Line by Teddy Slater, et al.
Subtraction Action by Loreen Leedy
Too Many Kangaroo Things to Do! by Stuart J. Murphy
Twizzlers Percentages Book by Jerry Pallotta

© McGraw-Hill Children's Publishing

0-7424-2698-X *Every Teacher Is a Reading Teacher: 101 Ways to Incorporate Reading into Your Classroom*

Name _____ Date _____

Retelling a Marvelous Math Story

Title of Book: _____

Author: _____

1. What is the setting for this story? _____

2. Who are the characters? What were they doing? _____
   _____

3. What is the problem in the story? _____

4. What are the actual numbers in the problem? _____

> **What math skills did the characters use to solve this problem? Circle any skills they used.**
>
> | | |
> |---|---|
> | Adding money amounts | Division |
> | Adding fractions | Looking for patterns |
> | Subtraction | Measuring |
> | Telling time | Weighing |
> | Counting by groups of numbers | Collecting Data |
> | Multiplication | Graphing |
> | Addition | Other _____ |

5. List the steps or events involved in solving the problem:

   a. _____

   b. _____

   c. _____

6. Do you think the characters made good choices in solving the problem? _____
   _____

7. Would you have solved the problem differently? Explain. ____
   _____

© McGraw-Hill Children's Publishing

0-7424-2698-X Every Teacher Is a Reading Teacher:
101 Ways to Incorporate Reading into Your Classroom

Special Projects

Teaching through special projects is one of the most effective ways to keep students enthusiastic about learning. Projects may be referred to as activities requiring more than one skill, incorporating two or more core content areas, focusing on the process, lasting over a length of time, with an ending goal in mind. Since projects involve lots of time and preparation, invite older students and parent volunteers to join in the fun!

2 Fun Fundraiser

Choose a destination for a field trip that corresponds with a science or social studies standard, such as a city museum or historical village. Keeping the destination within a three-hour drive will keep the trip manageable for younger students. Complete many of your fundraising efforts during math time. Allow several months for the fundraising. Appointed students or groups of students can work with you, an aid, or a parent to make transportation arrangements and calculate gas costs, meal costs, admissions costs, and any additional needs.

Before your trip, help students fill out a KWL chart about the place they are going to visit. Write three questions at the top of a sheet of chart paper divided into thirds: *What do you **know** about the place? What do you **want** to know about the place? What did you **learn** after we visited the place?* Have students fill out the first two sections of the chart. Then after the field trip or after visiting a Web site about a similar place, ask students to fill in the last section of the chart.

Know	Want to Know	Learn
*What do you **know** about the place?*	*What do you **want** to know about the place?*	*What did you **learn** after we visited/researched this place?)*

Encourage students to keep track of the amount of money needed for each student as well as for the total trip. Have them gather all the information, and then use a computer program to create spreadsheets or charts reporting the needed monies.

Help students practice using the business letter format to write letters to local businesses stating why the students think they would benefit from going on the trip. Have them ask the company to sponsor one or more children at a specific price per child or give a general donation. Have students keep track of the money as it comes in on their spreadsheets. Invite them to write thank-you notes as the money comes in and report to the company the amount raised as of that point.

After the trip, you may invite a representative from each sponsoring business to the school for coffee and cookies as students report what they learned from the trip!

Note: Many museums provide pre-teaching guides that can be helpful.

3 Run a Post Office
(Special Projects cont.)

Students will incorporate many reading, writing, and math skills in operating a school post office! This simple, yet engaging, project will introduce them to the principles of economics—needs and wants, products, expenses, profits, and the consumer/producer relationship. Begin the project by having students visit a local post office to see how they do business. There are many quality literature titles available describing the job of a mail carrier, the route of a letter, and how to write friendly letters. Some suggested titles include *The Jolly Postman* by Allan Ahlberg and *Mailing May* by Michael O. Tunnell.

After taking a trip to the post office and reading about mail delivery, brainstorm as a class how to go about running a school post office. List students' ideas on chart paper. Assign students specific jobs or have them fill out resumes and apply for jobs. Then help students do the following to get their post office up and running:

- Make a map of the school and decide how each room will be addressed. (Each class can take part in creating their own room/street name.)

- Determine the cost of creating postcards, stationery, and envelopes.

- Decide on a reasonable price to charge for postcard and letter stamps, stationery, postcards, and envelopes.

- Decide when the selling of stamps and mailing supplies will occur.

Give students time to design stamps and supplies. A cash register with a beginning till amount will be needed for making change. They can then create posters to hang throughout the school to advertise their post office. They should also write a letter to be distributed to all classrooms that states the times they will be selling stamps and the days the mail will be delivered. This information should also be put in the school newsletter. Students will use their own money for buying stamps.

Students can create a system to sort mail by hallway and then by classroom. Jobs may rotate every one to two weeks or every month. Once a month, the post office may run specials such as: "Buy one stamp, get one free!" "Read ten books and get 1/2 off!" Have your office managers keep track of the total number of stamps sold per day and per week. They can create a report to present to the math class as they make further decisions about how to run their business.

As soon as the post office opens, students throughout the school will be instantly motivated to write letters to their friends. Through this innovative activity, concepts of how to work with money are given real-life applications!

4. Run a Restaurant
(Special Projects cont.)

Invite students to create their own restaurant. Have them begin by reading menus donated from local restaurants. Introduce students to the idea of running a restaurant by assigning partners to read and practice ordering from menus. Next, have one student in each pair act as the server to record the items and the cost. Invite students to switch roles. Have them practice how to line up the decimal, explain their understanding of place value and carrying, and calculate the tax and tip. As students take orders, have them write short orders like taking notes in class. Invite them to come up with abbreviations for certain foods and special orders.

To set up a classroom restaurant, have students apply for different jobs, such as menu makers, managers, host/hostesses, servers or wait staff, cooks, decorators, table clearers, and so on. The menu makers can make menus with snack items and prices. They can write catchy phrases to describe and sell the items. Encourage students to go through the writing process as they plan, draft, proofread, and edit their menus. They can then publish them on the computer and add graphics to make the menus look professional. Make sure students have menu samples for reference. Point out special pictures, captions, and descriptive words that excite the senses! Have students choose items for the menu that require little actual cooking to keep the restaurant more manageable. Get families involved by having them donate prepared food items.

Next, create an advertising committee to make posters advertising the opening date, times, and prices of your restaurant. In addition, the managers will have to decide how many supplies to purchase, or get donated, so they are stocked for the event. The managers, or restaurant accountant, will also keep track of each committee's financial reports, so they can track each gain and loss. The hostess may want to pre-schedule, or make reservations for what time each class visits your restaurant. This will help students practice their skills at telling time and calculating elapsed time. The decoration committee may also use varying ABC shape patterns to decorate the borders of 11" x 14" paper for placemats. The cooks will have to use measurement skills to prepare some of the items using measuring spoons, cups, and ounce scales.

You may plan to run your restaurant as one-day activity or extend it to one day per month. Allowing the restaurant to operate several times allows students to experience different jobs and practice a variety of reading and math skills. The funds raised may be used toward the field trip fund or to purchase new math books for the classroom.

During the process of any project, there are sometimes discrepancies among the workers as to how to approach tasks or solve problems. Students can write problem-solving proposals suggesting how to solve a problem. They can read their proposals to the class, and then the class can take a vote on the best way to solve the problem!

5 Tall Tales

Read many tall tales to students, such as John Henry, Paul Bunyan, Mike Fink, and so on. Specifically discuss the number words used as literary devices to exaggerate and make the characters larger than life. For example, discuss Paul Bunyan's weight of 80 pounds at birth and the size of Babe, his blue ox. Babe grew to be about 24 axe handles wide between the eyes and ate 30 bales of hay as a snack. Have students create their own tall tales using large, yet realistic numbers to describe eating habits, strength, height, weight, and accomplishments achieved. A fun twist when writing is to encourage students to use family members as the main characters. The family member's accomplishments, current occupation, and facts about how his or her work has made the world a better place can be used as the basis for creating the main character. Make copies of the "Planning My Tall Tale" reproducible on page 14 for students to use in planning their stories.

Example:

Dave the Carpenter eats fourteen bowls of oatmeal for breakfast, four dozen eggs, and two gallons of milk. He lifts two cows for weights every morning. He built the largest home in the entire world. It covers 800 acres of land. There are 2,000 rooms and all the homeless now have a place to live!

Students will enjoy reading these stories to their families at open houses or parent conferences. Composing and reading tall tales is a wonderful way to encourage students to practice fluency and expression. The original stories can be taken home, but make sure to make copies to bind into a class *Tall Tales* book. When you create a class book, make sure to include a title page and table of contents. Each time a new class book is published, a different student or group of students can create the cover, title page, and table of contents.

Name _____ Date _____

Planning My Tall Tale

Use the Paul Bunyan story planner below to help create your own tall tale. Be sure to include numbers to exaggerate your character's traits.

My main character: _____

Occupation: _____

Setting(s): Where does your character live and work? _____
_____

What is the problem only your character can solve? _____
_____
_____
_____

What does your character eat for meals or snacks?
_____
_____
_____

What exercise or activity does your character do to stay strong? _____
_____
_____
_____

What does your character like to do? How can he/she do good for others using his/her strength and talent? _____
_____
_____
_____

Where does your character go? What does he/she accomplish? _____
_____
_____
_____

On a separate sheet of paper, plan your illustrations. One idea is to draw a picture of your character as a baby, draw your character eating or exercising, and then draw your character on the job completing an huge task.

© McGraw-Hill Children's Publishing

14

0-7424-2698-X Every Teacher Is a Reading Teacher: 101 Ways to Incorporate Reading into Your Classroom

6 Fantastic Fables

When teaching a unit on fables, you can integrate measurement using the story "The Tortoise and the Hare." Read several different versions of the fable. Note the differences in the style of text, vocabulary, and illustrations. Invite students to compare and contrast the stories and books. Point out that fables are special stories that have a moral or lesson. Ask them to identify the moral of the "The Tortoise and the Hare."

Then have students create their own racetrack based on the story. Require specific measurements for length and width, and a specific number of obstacles and corners to turn. Students can retell and act out these fables with mini-stuffed animals or toys. Make sure they identify the beginning, middle, and end of the story. They can also enlarge the measurements and work together to create a real-life racetrack on the playground. Invite students to figure out the finishing time of various animals.

7 It's a Mystery!

Solving problems in the genre of mysteries often involves mathematical calculations. Read mystery stories to students. Look for titles that tend to address skills in telling time at the scene of the crime, measuring distances, or tracking sequence of events. Have students record the evidence, the suspects, and the tools and skills used to solve the case on the "It's a Mystery!" reproducible on page 16. After reading and discussing several mystery stories, have students identify elements of the mystery genre and list them on the board.

Then have students use what they've learned about this genre to write their own mystery stories! Have them write in small groups, and then present their stories to the class. Periodically pause in the reading and ask the rest of the class to predict what might happen next.

Name _____ Date _____

It's a Mystery!

As you read a mystery book, record the skills the detectives or main characters used to solve the problem or crack the case. Look closely for the following: sequence of events, telling time, measuring, figuring out a riddle or clue, and general thinking skills.

Title of Mystery Book: _____

1. Where does this story take place? What is the setting?
   _____
   _____

2. What is the problem the characters have to solve?
   _____
   _____

3. What are the problem-solving skills used in this mystery book? Put a star by the math skills.

   a. _____
   b. _____
   c. _____
   d. _____
   e. _____

4. Would you be able to solve this mystery?   YES   NO

5. Do you have the skills the characters have?   YES   NO

6. Would you have solved the mystery differently? If yes, how?
   _____
   _____
   _____

© McGraw-Hill Children's Publishing

0-7424-2698-X *Every Teacher Is a Reading Teacher: 101 Ways to Incorporate Reading into Your Classroom*

8 Math Journals

Encourage each student to keep a math journal. A spiral notebook can have several uses in math class. It provides students with a common workspace to solve problems and record the steps used to solve problems. Students can also practice using complete sentences to explain their mathematical thinking processes. When students are solving problems, they can record in sentence form the steps they completed to find the answers. For example, when solving 25 + 47, a good answer would be: *First, I added the ones column, 7 + 5. The answer was 12. Next, I put a 2 in the ones column and put the 1 in the tens column. Last, I added 1 plus 2 plus 4 to get 7, or 7 tens. The answer is 72, 7 tens and 2 ones.* Point out that steps should be numbered or have students use sequencing words, such as first, second, third, then, next, and last.

At the end of each math period, encourage students to write one or more complete sentences to state what they learned or worked on that day. They can read their journals to their parents every Friday or at conference time. You may use students' journals as assessment tools to analyze whether or not students are grasping current concepts.

9 Five Little . . .

Use the familiar Halloween poem, "Five Little Pumpkins," to incorporate reading, math, and writing. Read the poem with students and point out the rhythm, rhyme, and patterns. Invite students to practice reading the ordinal words. Challenge them to see if they can come up with other rhyming words.

Copy the "Five Little Pumpkins" reproducible on page 18 for each student. Use it as a format for students to create their own poems! This activity helps students practice the reading, writing, and spelling of ordinal numbers. During this activity specific writing skills are addressed, such as using quotation marks, exploring possible rhyming words, and illustrating using speech bubbles. Students also practice speaking skills as they present their poems to the class. This activity can be used with any holiday, season, or setting. Each time you do this activity, the number of characters or objects can be increased.

© McGraw-Hill Children's Publishing

0-7424-2698-X *Every Teacher Is a Reading Teacher: 101 Ways to Incorporate Reading into Your Classroom*

Name _____ Date _____

Five Little Pumpkins

Five little pumpkins sitting on a gate.
The first one said, "Oh my, it's getting late!"
The second one said, "There are goblins in the air."
The third one said, "But we don't care."
The fourth one said, "Let's run, run, run."
The fifth one said, "Oh, it's just Halloween fun."
But ooooooo went the wind and out went their lights,
And the five little pumpkins rolled out of sight.

Plan Your Poem

_____ _____ _____ _____
   Number   Describing Word   Objects   Setting

The first one said, "_____"

The second one said, "_____"

The third one said, "_____"

The fourth one said, "_____"

The fifth one said, "_____"

_____

_____

When you publish your poem, remember to illustrate it. Draw each character or object. Use speech bubbles to show what they are saying.

© McGraw-Hill Children's Publishing   18   0-7424-2698-X *Every Teacher Is a Reading Teacher: 101 Ways to Incorporate Reading into Your Classroom*

10 Money Travels

Have students read about the process of making a dollar bill. Help them find information on the Internet to investigate this process. Then have them write a creative story about the route of a dollar or a larger bill. Have them include where it is spent and re-spent. Invite students to include several settings and characters that come in contact with the dollar. They can incorporate ideas such as whether or not a character needs the money to buy something important, or if the money is going to be spent on something fun. Before children write, brainstorm all the things one can buy with a dollar. Remind students that the dollar can also be combined with more money to buy more expensive items. Invite them to incorporate other fun, creative ideas. Maybe someone loses the dollar, a dog runs away with the dollar, or the dollar ends up being exchanged for foreign currency in another country.

Increase the challenge by having students write from the dollar's point of view. Point of view is an important literary element for students to understand. This approach can be used for most math tools. For example, students can write about what a clock thinks as it hangs on the wall in your classroom. What does it see, hear, and feel? What might a ruler say while it is being used for measurement?

11 Comparing Characters

Have students compare and contrast themselves with a character in a math story or other nonfiction story. Students could also read two stories and compare the main characters to each other. Comparing is both a math and literacy skill. Encourage the use of comparative and superlative adjectives like *good, better, best; tall, taller, tallest; happy, happier, happiest*. Brainstorm and list several examples on the board. Use a Venn diagram as a comparison tool for this writing piece.

Next, ask students to brainstorm topics for their own math books. Have them list story elements including setting, characters, main events, problem, and solution.

After writing, illustrating, and publishing their math books, have students share them with each other. Place the books in the class library for further enjoyment.

12 Persuasive Ads

During a unit on money, have students read the toy ads from newspapers or direct mail flyers. These are very easy to find, especially around the holidays. Have students read the advertisements and then record their top five choices of what they would like to purchase. Ask them to identify how the text and pictures helped to persuade them to make these choices. They should record the page, the name of the item, and the price. Then have them use their carrying skills to total the bill. Extend the addition with third graders by allowing them to use a calculator to figure out the tax.

13 Shape Town

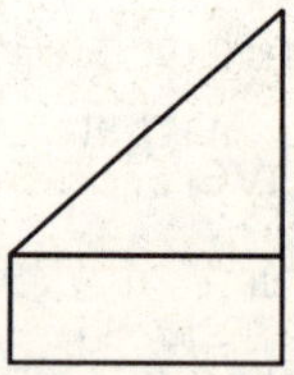

Invite students to build a shape town with "geo" blocks or three-dimensional blocks. Have students list all the characteristics for each block. For example: *a cube has six sides, twelve vertices, and eight edges.* Remind them that writing is always more interesting when it includes good describing words. Help them brainstorm and write possible words on the board: *big, small, round, square, red, blue, yellow,* and so on. Help students associate the printed words with the characteristics on actual blocks. Students can also write directions for how to build the town one block at a time. Remind them to use ordinal words or number the steps. Lastly, have them write a story about what occurs on a typical day in their shape town.

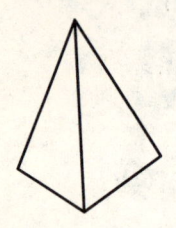

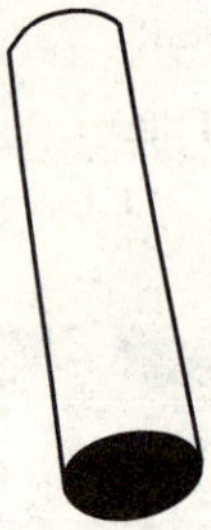

Along with the geometrical shape unit, have students describe the classroom using numbers and shapes. For example: "There are six hexagon-shaped tables. I see two rectangular prisms, one is a block and the other is a cracker box. The basketball is a sphere. There are three cylinders on the shelf; these are paper towels." Students can add positional words to their descriptions as well, such as: "The square book is **on** the round table. The cylinder-shaped pencil holder is **next to** the rectangular ruler." Provide a list of required geometric shapes and positional words for student reference.

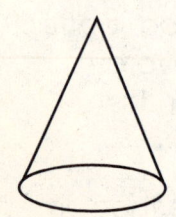

Once published, have students read their descriptions to an audience. The audience may consist of a small group of students, the whole class, another class, the principal, or family members.

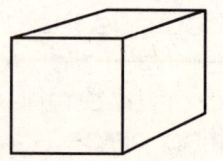

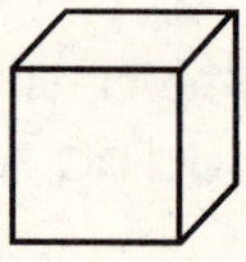

14 The Ideal Room

After studying a unit on standard measurement, have students create a map of their ideal classroom or bedroom. Have them draw a map with exact measurements of walls, closet length, bed dimensions, and other things they can creatively design using the scale one cm equals one foot. Show an example blueprint to students. Point out specific words and labels used and where they are located on the map. Guide students to see that these kinds of maps are aerial views or like they are looking down from a helicopter. Have students write a descriptive paragraph about their rooms including the measurements. Encourage them to explain why their room is ideal by pointing out the special features and the reasons they included them.

15 Write Your Own!

Have students read several counting books. As students read the books, they will expand their vocabulary. Discuss with students how the authors have incorporated counting into the stories. Then have students write their own counting books. Have students use one setting as the basis for their books. Encourage them to use colorful verbs, adjectives, and adverbs to describe the items being counted on each page. The simplicity of this writing project allows students a template for exploring quality descriptive writing vocabulary. Ask students to describe what the characters or objects are doing and create illustrations to match their descriptions. When the books are complete, use kindergarten or first grades as an audience.

Encourage the quality of word choices rather than the quantity. Use the book *Sea Squares* by Joy N. Hulme for students to see how the author uses ocean animals to describe the basic number of the objects, and also adds a group of items found on the creatures themselves. See the example below for a sample of this technique.

Example:
Two gray seals clapping their hands,
Eight flippers all on the sand.

16 Math Riddles

Have students write math riddles for their classmates to read and solve. Show students how to write clues to provide just enough, but not too much information. Give a few examples on the board and point out important clue words, such as more than, less than, equal to, same as, and so on. Have students write three clues to describe a number and then ask a question.

Example:
I am 25 more than two quarters.
I am 25 less than $1.00.
Use me to buy a juice in the juice machine.
What number am I?

17 Eleven and Twelve

Read aloud the book *12 Ways to Get to 11* by Eve Merriam. Point out the importance of illustration in this book and how it helps students visualize the concepts. Have students follow the book's format to write a class book of *12 Ways to Get to 11*. First, divide the class into twelve groups. Ask each group to complete a page for the story. They will need to decide on a setting, as well as the combinations of objects to include. Have them write four to six sentences describing the setting and the number of each object in the setting. Remind students that their illustrations are critical for readers to visualize the text.

18 What Is a Dozen?

Using *A Dozen Dizzy Dogs* by William H. Hooks, have students insert the word *dozen* after every number word listed. For example: *One **dozen** dizzy dogs, digging all alone. Two **dozen** dizzy dogs, digging up a bone.* Have students figure out which numeral each group of dozens equals. This will reinforce the multiplication x12 math facts. Have each student or pair of students illustrate one page with the new sentence, and record the multiplication fact used.

19 Frozen Treat Sale

After reading a book about summer or frozen treats invite students to have their own frozen treat sale! Have them do some planning ahead of time like they did for the "Run a Post Office" and "Run a Restaurant" activities on pages 11 and 12. This project, however, takes much less planning. Students will need to price out the amount of supplies needed, make posters to advertise the sale, and be able to take money and count back change for purchases. Help students do some research on how to write effective ads by looking through the newspaper and food magazines. Review good advertising techniques and persuasive writing. Food advertisements usually include lots of great sensory describing words. List some of these on the board for student reference. Suggest that students use their profits to purchase more math books for the classroom or school library!

20 Readers' Theater

Another genre that can be addressed in math class is the play. Have students read plays describing how the characters had issues with shopping (money), cooking (measurement), sharing equal pieces with friends (fractions), or possibly being late for a big event (time). Review the vocabulary featured in these stories, especially math-related vocabulary, such as terms dealing with money, measurement, and time. If already produced resources are not available, help students write their own short plays using the "Readers' Theater" reproducible on page 24. They can work in small groups to write the text and design props. This is a good opportunity for a buddy project with an older class.

21 Favorite Athletes

Invite students to research their favorite athletes. Have them use books, sports magazines, the sports page in the newspaper, and the Internet to find information. All of an athlete's stats are recorded and make great applications for connecting reading and math. Have students write short reports that include the player's birthday, age, average hours they practice per week, and statistics for number of points scored or accomplishments achieved. Students can also find and summarize the rules of the game. Have them present their reports to the class. This project can be extended to research two players in the same sport and league and mathematically compare their statistics.

Name _____ Date _____

Readers' Theater

Write your own play about math. Remember, the characters have to use their math skills to solve the problem!

Examples of Problems:

A child needs to buy something and doesn't have enough money.

There is one pizza and four children. How can they share equally?

Keep the story very simple. Remember to write using a play format. Start with an introduction of the setting and time. Introduce the characters. Then write exactly what each character says after his or her name. Use the planning sheet below to get started.

Title: _____

Narrator: _____

Problem: _____

Setting: _____

Characters: _____
_____
_____

Events:

1. _____
2. _____
3. _____

Solution: _____

Math Skills Used:
_____
_____

22 Math Vocabulary Lists

Incorporate math vocabulary into daily lessons. Identify a math word for each day or week, and invite students to keep math mini-dictionaries. Show students how vocabulary words are recorded in dictionaries. Tell them to leave space in their dictionaries for a diagram or example to explain each word. They can also write each word on a 3" x 5" index card to put in alphabetical order on a metal ring. Have children practice their dictionary skills by looking up the math words in a children's dictionary. Create a list of math vocabulary words required for your grade level, district, or state standards. A good resource for creating the list is to personally take a practice math state educational assessment profile. Record all of the new or challenging direction or math words. After making a list, find words with common links based on specific math concepts. Separate the words into lists of five to eight words.

Each week, students can go through a process to study the words. The first week, they can read and correctly pronounce the words. The second week, they can study the spelling of the words. The third week, they can memorize the definition of and an example for each word. Use the "Math Vocabulary List" on pages 26 and 27 to get started.

23 Grandfather Tang's Tangrams

Read aloud the book *Grandfather Tang's Story* by Ann Tompert. Then invite students to use tangrams for a series of follow-up activities. Tangrams can be purchased at most teacher supply stores or through toy store catalogs. They can also be reproduced and cut from colorful card stock or tagboard. All seven pieces should fit into one square. Pre-outlined shapes are also available, so students have a guide for building characters and objects. Allow students time to explore building various shapes and objects. Manipulating tangrams develops students' visual and spatial awareness, providing benefits similar to those of completing a challenging jigsaw puzzle.

Have students create a simple story using basic story elements and tangrams. Students can manipulate the pieces as they share their stories, or they may use another set of seven pieces each time a different character speaks. They can use a third set to create an object in the setting. Encourage students to practice their story presentations many times, and then write the story on paper. They can fill in a simple story map as a guide for the presentation, and then transfer the story from the story map into sentences and paragraphs. Have students glue the card stock tangrams on each final page as illustrations. They can draw the background and setting around the tangram pieces. After students present their stories, encourage them to be guest storytellers in other classrooms. Invite them to first discuss tangrams, and then to present their stories.

Math Vocabulary List

PROBABILITY
always
chance
equally likely
fifths
fourths
fraction
half
impossible
less likely
more likely
never
possible
probability
sort
tally
thirds
whole

GEOMETRY
circle
cone
congruent
corner
cube
cylinder
edge
equal
flip
line of symmetry
prism
pyramid
reflection
side
surface
symmetry
triangle
vertex
vertices

GRAPHING
bar graph
category
collection
column
data
display
equal
frequency
frequency table
horizontal
least

less
more
most
one
pictograph
picture graph
real graph
repeat
row
same
sort
table
tally
vertical

NUMBER SENSE/PATTERNS
after
alike
before
bigger
different
down
color
compare
count
create
digit
equals (=)
fact family
follows
greater than (>)
growing patterns
hundreds chart
larger
less than (<)
next
number lines
numeral
order
pattern
place value
repeat
reproduce
sequence
shape
shrinking patterns
size
skip count
smaller
up
variable

CALCULATOR
constant feature
enter
ON/C
operation signs

MEASUREMENT
abbreviations
balance scale
beginning point
capacity
centimeter
cups
customary (US)
end point
estimate
feet
foot
gallon
greater
heavier
height
inch
kilogram
kilometer
length
less
lighter
liter
mass
measure
meter
metric measure
mile
millimeter
nearest
ounce
pint
pound
quart
ruler
standard measure
tablespoon
tape measure
teaspoon
volume
weight
width
unit
yardstick

Math Vocabulary List (cont.)

TEMPERATURE
below
boiling
Celsius scale (C)
degrees (°)
Fahrenheit scale (F)
fives
freezing
thermometer

MONEY
bill
cash
change
cents (¢)
coins
decimal
dime
dollar ($)
half-dollar
heads
nickel
penny
quarter
tails
value

MULTIPLICATION/DIVISION
array
commutative property
digit
divide
dividend
division sign (÷)
division table
divisor
equation
fact family
factor
hundreds place
manipulatives
multiplication sign (×)
multiplication table
multiplier
multiply
number sentence problem
ones column/ones place
product

quotient
solution
tens column/tens place
times
twice
word problem

ADDITION/SUBTRACTION
add
addend
addition facts
addition sign (+)
altogether
associative property
base ten
column
commutative property
difference
digits
equal
equation
estimate
even
how many
how much
hundreds
identity property
in all
minus
ones
place value
plus
problem
regroup
rounding
subtract
subtraction facts
subtraction sign (–)
sum
total
trade

PLACE VALUE
after
before
between
equal to
even

greater than
less than
odd
ones
tens
thousands

FRACTIONS
half
halves
denominator
eighths
fifths
fourths
greater than
less than
numerator
order
parts
sixths
thirds
whole

TELLING TIME
afternoon
a.m.
colon (:)
digital clock
early
elapsed time
evening
half past
hour
hour hand
interval
late
midnight
minute hand
morning
night
noon
o'clock
on the hour
p.m.
quarter past
quarter to
second
second hand

24 Math Story Problems

Reading and solving math story problems involves critical reading and analysis skills, as well as the application of general mathematical principles. Teach students to read all the information in the problem and then decipher which facts are necessary for finding the answer. Students should also become familiar with key words and vocabulary to look for when deciding which operation to use. Get students started by having them complete the "Solve It! Word Problems" reproducible on page 29.

Encourage students to explain their strategies, such as: "First, I read the problem. Then I read the problem again and decided what information I needed to solve the problem and which operation to use. I wrote down the beginning number. Then I used the operation to come up with the answer. I drew a picture to help me solve the problem."

Students can use a marker to highlight key numbers and words. They should also write down the steps they used to solve problems. After working to solve several story problems, they will progress to writing their own. Show students how to write a rough draft and a final copy with an illustration. Bind children's word problems into a class book to keep with the other math books.

As students grasp a complete understanding of the elements and strategies involved, word problems can become increasingly complex. Students can learn to add additional information in a sentence that will not be needed to solve the problem. For example, when writing a problem that involves an amount of money to be calculated, include the character's age, the setting, or the date of the event.

Using a special holiday or seasonal theme is great way to get students motivated and keep the learning fun. When writing these problems students can list the number of objects in the setting in groups. This can help incorporate multiplication facts. For example, if the theme is winter, students could write problems like the examples below.

Examples:

Troy built 4 snowmen with 3 balls each. How many balls did he use all together?

There are 6 friends skiing at Grizzly Bear Ski Lodge. How many skis are there in all?

Mattie made 5 mugs of hot chocolate. She put 4 marshmallows in each mug. How many marshmallows were in all the cups?

Name _____   Date _____

Solve It! Word Problems

Read each word problem. Decide what information you need to solve it. Use the space under the problem to show your work. Write your final equation and answer on the line.

1. Lindsey has 567 beads to make jewelry. Tessa has 576 beads to make jewelry. Who has more? (Hint: Write a math sentence using <, >, or = to compare and show your answer.)

   _____

2. If Anthony eats half of a pizza that has 8 pieces, how many pieces did he eat? (Hint: Draw a picture and write a fraction.)

   _____

3. Natalie and Taryn collect marbles. Taryn has 62 marbles. Natalie has 26 marbles. Who has more? How many more?

   _____

4. Devin's soccer game starts in 1 hour and 15 minutes. The time is 8:15. What time does the game start?

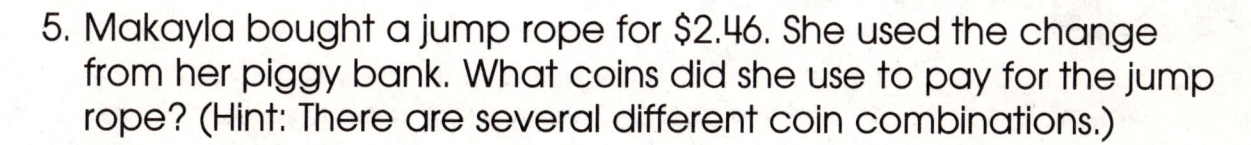

   _____

5. Makayla bought a jump rope for $2.46. She used the change from her piggy bank. What coins did she use to pay for the jump rope? (Hint: There are several different coin combinations.)

   _____

25 Singing Math

Singing is an effective way to incorporate the musical intelligence in order to grasp mathematical concepts while simultaneously reading lyrics. Write the words to some songs on chart paper or sentence strips to place in a pocket chart. Use different colors to emphasize number words and matching colors to highlight rhyming words. Point to each word as you sing with students. Use motions or hand gestures to help students remember the words of the songs.

As students become familiar with the songs, they will begin to recognize new words. Write new words on index cards for students to read independently or add to their math dictionaries. Have students write the lyrics in their math journals, so they can practice reading and singing the songs after completing assignments. Make songbooks to keep in the math center. Invite students to check out songbooks, so they can take them home and sing songs with their families.

Include songs about the months and seasons, addition and subtraction, money, fractions, multiplication and division, skip counting, telling time, or other required concepts. Copy the "Math Songs to Read and Sing!" reproducibles on pages 31 and 32 for students to place in math song folders. Have students illustrate the concepts in the songs on a separate sheet of paper. Students may also work with a partner to use familiar tunes for writing their own songs featuring math concepts or facts.

Suggested Titles for Singing in Math
"Can Cockatoos Count by Twos?" by Hap Palmer
"Months on the Move" by Hap Palmer
"A Penny" Disney Silly Songs
"Numbers Everywhere" by Kevin Kameraad, author of *The Tomato Collection*
"Rhythms on Parade" by Hap Palmer

26 Math Poetry

Invite students to read math poetry. The rhythm and rhyme will help reinforce important math concepts and vocabulary. Many jump-rope rhymes include counting and number words. Invite students to choose favorite poems to read or act out for the class while identifying number and rhyming words.

Name _____ Date _____

Math Songs to Read and Sing!

Read and sing the following songs to reinforce counting. Write the matching numeral above each number word.

Counting by Twos
(Sing to the tune "Twinkle, Twinkle, Little Star.")

Two, Four, Six, Eight, Ten, Twelve,

Fourteen, Sixteen, Eighteen, Twenty.

Counting by Fives
(Sing to the tune "You're a Grand Old Flag.")

Five, Ten, Fifteen, Twenty,
    Twenty-five, Thirty,

Thirty-five, Forty, Forty-five,
    Fifty, Fifty-five,

Sixty, Sixty-five, Seventy,
    Seventy-five, Eighty,

Eighty-five, Ninety, Ninety-five,
    One Hundred.

I can count by fives all the
    way to one hundred!

Name _____ Date_____

Math Songs to Read and Sing!

Counting by Threes
(Sing to the tune "Polly Wolly Doodle.")

Three, Six, Nine, Twelve, Fifteen, Eighteen, Twenty-one,

I can count by threes!

Twenty-four, Twenty-seven, Thirty, Thirty-three, Thirty-six

I can count by threes!

I can count. I can count. I can count by threes.

I can count. I can count. Won't you count with me?

Counting by Fours
(Clap for the three skipped numbers, and say the fourth number like a rap or chant.)

Clap, clap, clap, 4!   Clap, clap, clap, 8!   Clap, clap, clap, 12!

Clap, clap, clap, 16! Clap, clap, clap, 20! Clap, clap, clap, 24!

Clap, clap, clap, 28! Clap, clap, clap, 32! Clap, clap, clap, 36!

Clap, clap, clap, 40! Clap, clap, clap, 44! Clap, clap, clap, 48!

Counting by Tens
(Sing to the tune "Eensy, Weensy Spider.")

Ten, Twenty, Thirty, Forty, Fifty, Sixty,

Seventy, Eighty, Ninety, One Hundred.

© McGraw-Hill Children's Publishing

0-7424-2698-X *Every Teacher Is a Reading Teacher: 101 Ways to Incorporate Reading into Your Classroom*

27 Math Careers

Have students read and research different occupations, recording which ones require math skills. Help them to create a chart or graph to organize their information. Invite guest speakers to share with students how they use math in their jobs. Ask them to bring in any measuring or math tools they use while working. Encourage speakers to tell students about special words or terms they use in their jobs while you list them on the board. Be sure to discuss these terms later in the day. Students can also take notes while the speaker is presenting. Suggested occupations include: accountant, banker, builder, homemaker, artist, musician/composer, contractor, electrician, doctor/veterinarian, baker/chef, politician, seamstress, metalworker, cashier, and architect. You can even invite your principal!

28 Math Routine

Post a math routine in the classroom every day before math class. Have students read this information daily. This can be used as another tool for reinforcing math vocabulary. Your routine may look like the list below.

Randomly choose someone's name from a basket of name cards to begin the routine. The chosen student then picks a name card for the next job, and so on.

- *Add a number to the calendar. How many more days are left in this month?*
- *Name the current weather and record the temperature on the chart. Chart the weather conditions on the bar or line graph.*
- *Point to the correct number on the hundreds chart as we sing, counting by twos, threes, fours, fives, and tens.*
- *Add a number to the number of days in school.*
- *Add a nickel to the number that represents the amount of days in school.*
- *Add a base ten block to the number of the day.*
- *Sing a math song from a CD or tape.*
- *Solve the story problem on the board.*
- *Think about the math vocabulary word of the day or week. Spell it in your head. Tell a friend what it means.*
- *Listen to (teacher's name) read the math story of the day.*
- *Follow the directions to complete your math work and activities.*

Modify the directions every four to six weeks to keep students' interest.

Another way to integrate reading and math is to use a math message. A math message is a sentence written on the overhead or board. You can use the message to communicate the agenda or plan for the day and then pose a story problem for students to work on independently or with a partner.

29 Math Games

Math games are valuable tools for applying and practicing math concepts. Help students read the directions and then challenge them to figure out how to play the game. Some suggested math games that can be purchased at most toy stores include: Monopoly or Monopoly Junior, S'math, Life, Sorry, Trouble, Connect Four, 10,000, and Dominos. You can also introduce students to a variety of simple card games, which reinforce number values.

Have students use the "Make a Math Game" reproducible on page 35 to create their own math games! First, they need to decide on the math skill that will be reinforced and practiced in the game. Then, they will write directions for how to play the game. Invite students to work in pairs. They could even use a game board from another game and write new rules.

30 Numbers About My State

Invite students to research information about their state and create a report or book. Show them how to research relevant and interesting facts using books, encyclopedias, newspapers, and the Internet. Have students specifically look for number data about their state. For example: length and width in miles, number of lakes, population, average income, largest lake, distances from one city to another, tallest mountain, and so on. These kinds of facts will appear in captions for tables, diagrams, photos, and charts. Demonstrate how to read and analyze visuals. Have students use the "Numbers About My State" reproducible on page 36 to plan their writing. Invite them to present their reports or books in small groups.

31 Spider Crackers

Use simple recipes for teaching measurement, fractions, temperature, and for reading and following directions. Point out that directions are sequenced with numbers and ordinal words. Have students read the directions for making spider crackers on page 37. Ask them to summarize the directions in their own words. Encourage them to follow the directions without any assistance. They can compare results when everyone is finished. Other easy recipes you can use include: punch (liquid measurement), no-bake chocolate cookies, and no-bake peanut butter balls (measuring cups and spoons).

As an extension, have students create their own food bug, animal, or object. They can build the creation and then write directions for a friend to follow.

32 Math Is Everywhere!

Have students interview family members about the importance of math skills in their daily lives and in their jobs. Invite students to work on this project over two weeks and then bring in their findings. Make a class graph showing which skills are used most and least. Use the "Math Is Everywhere! Interview Sheet" on page 38.

Name _____ Date _____

Make a Math Game

Write your own rules for a new math game.

Title of the Game: _____

Number of Players: _____

Materials Needed: _____
_____
_____

What is the object/goal of the game? _____
_____
_____

How to Play:

1. _____

2. _____

3. _____

4. _____

5. _____

6. _____

7. _____

8. _____

9. _____

10. _____

Name _____ Date _____

Numbers About My State

1. My state's name is _____.

2. There are about _____ people who live in my state.

3. My state is _____ miles long and _____ miles wide.

4. My state was established in the year _____.

5. My state flag is _____.

6. My state is known for _____.

7. The highest mountain in my state is _____.
   It is _____ feet tall.

8. The capital of my state is _____.

9. I live _____ miles from the capitol.

10. The longest bridge in my state is _____ miles long. The bridge is named _____.

11. The average temperature in spring is _____.

12. The average temperature in summer is _____.

13. The average temperature in winter is _____.

14. The average temperature in fall is _____.

15. Last year, it rained _____ inches.

16. Another fact about my state is _____
_____.

© McGraw-Hill Children's Publishing

0-7424-2698-X *Every Teacher Is a Reading Teacher: 101 Ways to Incorporate Reading into Your Classroom*

Name _____ Date _____

Spider Crackers

Check the boxes as you gather your material and ingredients. Then check the boxes as you complete the directions.

Materials:
- ❑ small paper plates
- ❑ plastic knives

Ingredients:
- ❑ round crackers (two per student)
- ❑ small pretzel sticks
- ❑ three to five small jars of peanut butter (one for each table of students)
- ❑ chocolate chips (eight per student)

Directions:
- ❑ 1. Spread peanut butter on a round cracker.
- ❑ 2. Press eight pretzel "legs" into the peanut butter, four on each side.
- ❑ 3. Spread peanut butter on another cracker. Put the cracker on top of the pretzel legs, peanut butter side down.
- ❑ 4. Put a small dab of peanut butter on the front of the top cracker.
- ❑ 5. Press six chocolate chips into the peanut butter to look like eyes.
- ❑ 6. Leave your spider on the plate so you can compare it to the others at your table.

How are the spider crackers the same? How are they different?

_____

_____

Eat and enjoy! Yum!

Name _____ Date _____

Math Is Everywhere! Interview Sheet

Choose an adult to interview. Ask how this person uses math skills in everyday life. Encourage the person to give at least three examples. You will have one week to gather information. Bring your interview sheet back to school on _____. We will make a class graph to show which types of math skills are used most and least.

Math Skills

money	multiplication	volume
carrying	division	capacity
borrowing	addition	weight
fractions	subtraction	distance
patterns	telling time	telling temperature
greater than/less than	measurement	reading/making graphs
skip counting	length	

Sample Interview

"Hi, mom! May I ask you a few questions? Now that you are an adult, when do you use math? Do you use math at your job? I know you have to think about money. Can you tell me what math skills you use to work with money? How do you use math at home?"

Continue by asking about other math skills listed in the box above. Find out when and how these skills are used.

Name of Adult: _____

1. Math skill: _____

   When and how: _____

2. Math skill: _____

   When and how: _____

3. Math skill: _____

   When and how: _____

© McGraw-Hill Children's Publishing

SCIENCE AND TECHNOLOGY

33 Science Literature Circles

Find picture books, stories, nonfiction and informative books, biographies, and novels about science and science-related topics or people. Help students form science literature circles. Arrange students into small groups—four students usually work best. The group chooses a selection to read. Ask each group to read a different selection about the same topic. The group reads their selection and discusses the material. Afterward, hold a class discussion about the topic. Ask each group to present what they learned from the selection they read. Guide the discussion to help students compare and contrast different perspectives on the topic presented in each selection.

Basic Features of Science Circles

- Students form small, temporary groups.
- Each group reads different material about the same topic.
- Groups meet to discuss the material.
- Groups take notes about their discussions.
- Discussions focus on the material and what has been learned about the topic but are not overly structured.
- When reading and discussion is finished, groups share what they have learned with the class.

Display a variety of science books and other materials in the classroom. See the suggested reading list on page 40 for group selections. Also, try searching the National Science Teachers Association Web site for a list of Outstanding Trade Books for Students K–12.

Suggested Titles for Science

The age ranges and levels of these books vary. Use them according to students' needs, interests, and abilities.

Birds Build Nests by Yvonne Winer
The Drop in My Drink: The Story of Water on Our Planet by Meredith Hooper
Earthquakes by Franklyn M. Branley
Exploring Deserts by Barbara J. Behm and Veronica Bonar
Floratorium by Joanne Oppenheim
From Egg to Butterfly by Shannon Zemlicka
Giant Pandas by Gail Gibbons
Girls Who Looked Under Rocks: The Lives of Six Pioneering Naturalists by Jeannine Atkins
Great Black Heroes: Five Brilliant Scientists by Lynda Jones
I Want to Be an Environmentalist by Stephanie Maze and Catherine O'Neill Grace
The International Space Station by Franklyn M. Branley
Ladybugs: Red, Fiery, and Bright by Mia Posada
The Magic School Bus Lost in the Solar System by Joanna Cole
Mistakes That Worked by Charlotte Foltz Jones
The Ocean by Mel Higginson
Ocean Day by Shelley Rotner and Ken Kreisler
Our Big Home: An Earth Poem by Linda Glaser
Our Planet Earth (101 Questions and Answers) by Steve Parker
Questions and Answers About Polar Animals by Michael Chinery
The Science Book of Hot and Cold by Neil Ardley
The Science Book of Magnets by Neil Ardley
The Sun, the Wind, and the Rain by Lisa Westberg Peters
Temperature and You by Betsy Maestro, et al.
To Fly: The Story of the Wright Brothers by Wendie Old
The Very First Dinosaurs by Dougal Dixon
Weather and Climate (Young Discoverers: Geography Facts and Experiments) by Barbara Taylor
Your Amazing Senses: 36 Games, Puzzles, and Tricks by Ron Van Der Meer, et al.

© McGraw-Hill Children's Publishing

0-7424-2698-X *Every Teacher Is a Reading Teacher: 101 Ways to Incorporate Reading into Your Classroom*

34 Detecting Details

Invite small groups of students to work together as detectives. Before students read a chapter in their textbooks, write five questions on the board that require students to find facts from the text. For example: *What is the name of the process that occurs when liquid changes into a gas?* Try to use the same terminology as the text, so words will look familiar when students are skimming. Instruct students to skim the text in the chapter to find the information and look at the pictures, diagrams, and bolded or italicized words. Students can work in groups or individually. This activity helps familiarize students with the chapter while providing practice in skimming and noting important text features like headings, sidebars, captions, labels, vocabulary, maps, and diagrams.

35 Facing Facts

Invite students to read magazines to search for science content. There are numerous magazines devoted to science and scientific concepts, such as: *Ranger Rick, Zoobooks, National Geographic for Kids,* and *Ask Magazine.*

Use the "Fact and Opinion" reproducible on page 42 to help students distinguish between fact and opinion. After reading a science article, discuss with students the difference between a fact and an opinion.

Example:

Fact: Something that has actually happened or is true; a fact can be proven

Opinion: A personal belief based on what seems to be true; feelings about a topic

Provide students with some examples of each. Then ask them to select important statements from the material and decide if each is a fact or an opinion. Instruct students to write each statement in the appropriate column on the reproducible.

Name _____ Date _____

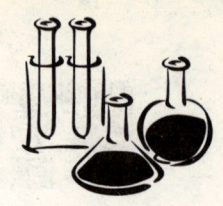

Fact and Opinion

Read the article your teacher gave you. Choose the most important statements from the article. Decide if each statement is a fact or an opinion. Write the statement in the correct column below.

Fact: Something that has actually happened or is true; a fact can be proven. For example: *Killer whales travel in pods.*

Opinion: A personal belief based on what seems to be true; feelings about a topic or event. For example: *Albert Einstein is the greatest scientist in history.*

Fact	Opinion

36 Science Journals

Prompt students to write in science journals. After reading an article or from a textbook, ask students to write a short summary of what they read. Remind them to include the main idea of the selection and details that support the main idea. Rewriting learned concepts and ideas helps build comprehension and reinforces memory. As an alternative, ask students to write in their science journals about some of the topics below.

- What did you learn today?
- What else would you like to know about this topic?
- Explain the concept we discussed today.
- Describe what you (or your group) accomplished today.
- Record your observations of the experiment.
- Record the data you discovered today.
- Record vocabulary words you want to remember.
- Encourage students to read their science journals often. Journals are useful tools when reviewing for a test or building up to new concepts.

37 New Discoveries

New scientific discoveries and events are often highly publicized. For example, new revelations from space exploration or advances in medicine are usually prominently featured in newspapers and magazines. Urge students to consult science articles to find out more about these discoveries. Refer to children's magazines such as *National Geographic for Kids* and *Time for Kids* to find information about current scientific discoveries.

Teach students to understand the usefulness of publishing scientific findings in these periodicals. Ask students, "What purpose does it serve for the general public?" Have students evaluate the effectiveness and purpose of the article. Ask, "Does the article give adequate information for the reader?" "What is lacking?" "Is the article intended for informational purposes, entertainment, persuasion, or to enhance our culture?" "How well does the article fulfill its purpose?" Hold a class discussion on these questions, or ask students to write their thoughts in their science journals.

The article may serve as a springboard for further research or to stimulate interest for a project or investigation. Foster this excitement and encourage students to deepen their understanding.

38 Vocabulary Stretchers

Before reading any selection such as a textbook, article, or experiment directions, have students preview the material for challenging vocabulary words. Make copies of the "Vocabulary Preview" on page 45 for students. Next, organize students into small groups. Invite group members to skim the material and write down any words that are unfamiliar or they do not understand. Then, ask them to make an educated guess about the meaning of each word. Remind them to use context clues, root words, affixes, or any other strategy to help them figure out possible meanings.

Invite each group to tell which words they found difficult. Write the words on a sheet of chart paper or word-wall cards. Discuss the words that appear most frequently and brainstorm possible meanings for each word. Prompt groups to talk about how they arrived at a possible meaning for the word.

Then ask students to go back and find the actual definition for the words on their lists. Instruct them to write the definitions on their papers. Encourage students to keep the papers in a convenient location for easy reference while reading. Make sure all students understand the vocabulary before reading the selection.

39 Starting with the Roots

Teach students how to use common root words, prefixes, and suffixes to help them figure out unfamiliar words they encounter while reading. Show them how to break apart words and find familiar parts. When they find a part of a word for which they know the meaning, they can use inferencing to figure out a possible meaning for the entire word. Help students with the "Starting with the Roots" reproducible on page 46 to practice affixes and stretch their vocabularies. Keep a running list of these word parts posted in the classroom for student reference during future science readings.

Extend this activity by categorizing and alphabetizing challenging science terminology before reading a new chapter or unit. Select ten words for students to put in alphabetical order. Practice using dictionaries to write out the definitions and identify their roots and affixes. While reading the chapter together, refer to the definitions and word parts to help students with fluency.

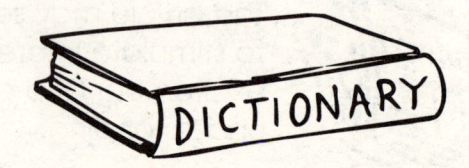

Name _____ Date _____

Vocabulary Stretchers

Skim the selection you are about to read. Write down any words you don't know. Carefully look at the word to find any clues about the meaning, such as parts you already know, context clues from the sentence, or picture clues. Write a possible meaning for the word. Finally, look up the definition in the glossary or dictionary, and write it in the definition box.

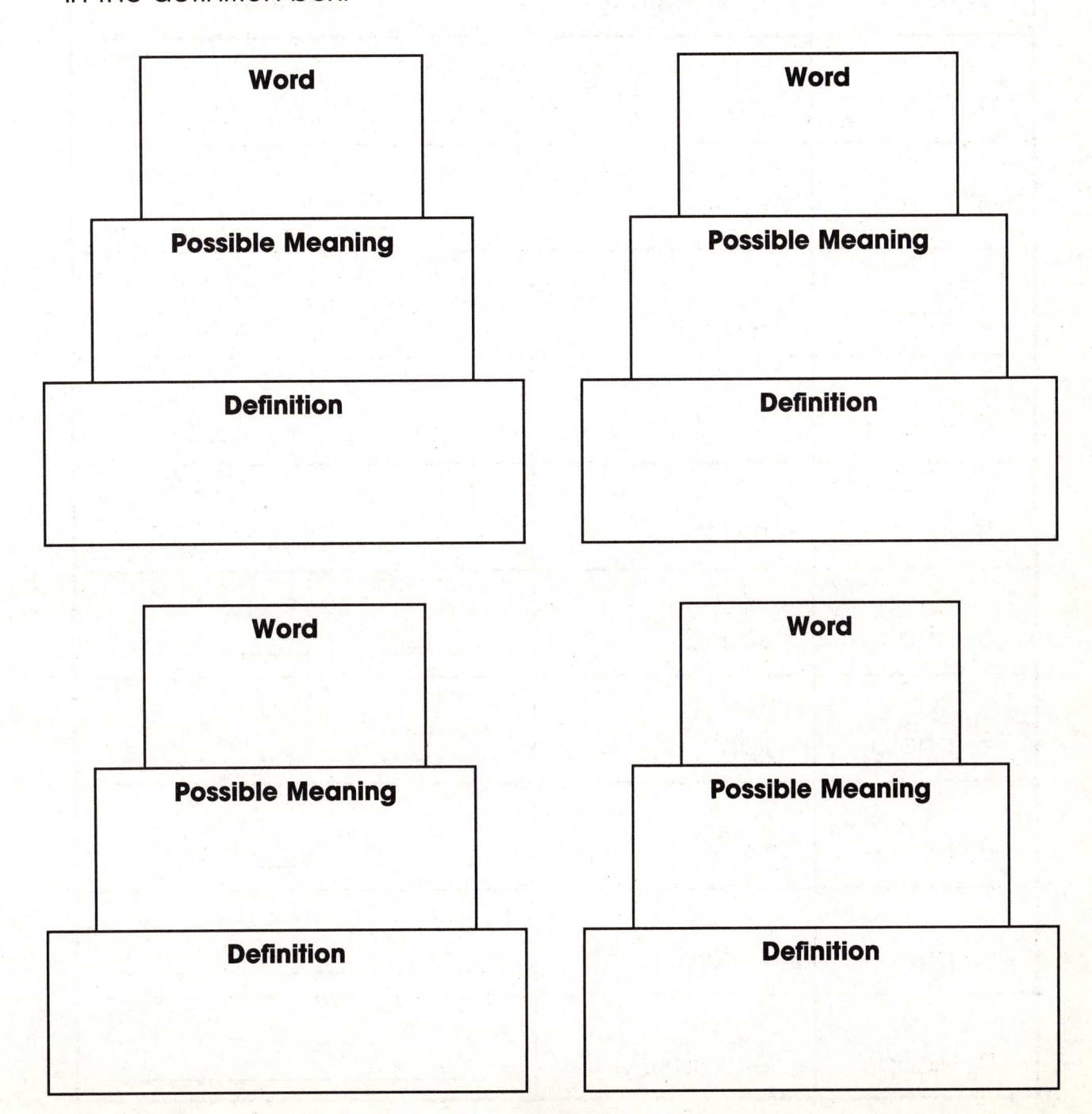

Word

Possible Meaning

Definition

Word

Possible Meaning

Definition

Word

Possible Meaning

Definition

Word

Possible Meaning

Definition

Name _____ Date _____

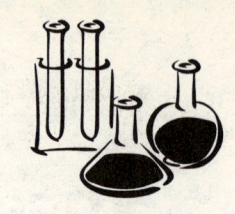

Starting with the Roots

Read the root words, prefixes, and suffixes below. Think of a science word that contains part of the word. Write the full word on the line.

Example: Geo-   earth   *geology*

Word Part	Meaning	Example
1. bio-	life	_____
2. hydro-	water	_____
3. inter-	between	_____
4. -ology	the study of	_____
5. lunar	moon	_____
6. phono-	sound	_____
7. photo-	light	_____
8. micro-	small	_____
9. pre-	before	_____
10. -scope	examine, view	_____

© McGraw-Hill Children's Publishing

0-7424-2698-X *Every Teacher Is a Reading Teacher: 101 Ways to Incorporate Reading into Your Classroom*

40 Nominate a Scientist

Have students select a prominent scientist they would like to nominate to a Scientist Hall of Fame. They can select from the list below or choose someone else they admire.

Instruct students to conduct research to learn about the scientist's life and scientific discoveries, using the Internet, encyclopedias, and books from the library. Have them complete the "Scientist Nomination Form" on page 48. They can draw a picture or photocopy a photo from a reference book to fill in the picture box. Finally, invite volunteers to share their nominations with the class. Hold a mock election to choose five entrants into a Scientist Hall of Fame. Post the nomination forms on a special bulletin board, so the whole class can learn about scientific landmarks and the scientists who discovered them.

Scientists to Study

- Rachel Carson
- George Washington Carver
- Nicolaus Copernicus
- Marie Curie
- Charles Darwin
- Albert Einstein
- Galileo Galilei
- Jane Goodall
- Alexander Fleming
- Diane Fossey
- William Harvey
- Ernest Just
- Maria Mayer
- Dmitri Mendeleev
- Gregor Mendel
- Sir Isaac Newton
- Charles Turner

Name _____ Date _____

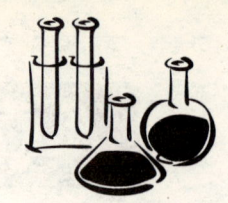

Scientist Nomination Form

Name of scientist: _____

Birth date: _____

Birthplace: _____

Branch of science: _____

Important discoveries: _____

How did this person change the world? _____
_____

Write three questions you would like to ask this scientist:

1. _____
2. _____
3. _____

41 Science Snippets

After reading about a science concept, invite students to write a found poem on the topic. Found poems are derived from the text students read. Since all the lines of the poem come from the reading selection, students do not need to add any words of their own. This makes it a great exercise for reluctant poets.

Ask students to choose the seven sentences they think are the most important from the reading selection. Have them write the sentences on the brainstorming part of the "Science Snippets" reproducible on page 50. Then ask them to underline or highlight the words and phrases from the sentences that really capture the essence of the concept. They will use these words and phrases to write the poem.

Instruct students to arrange the words and phrases in a way that best captures the meaning of the idea or concept. Words or phrases can be repeated for emphasis. The poems can be any length, but a minimum of six lines gives students a guideline. Encourage students to be creative, while retaining the scientific integrity of the concept.

42 Survival Kits

Have students read about living organisms and their basic needs. Discuss how each need is vital to the creature's survival. Then have students create how-to pamphlets about caring for a living creature with sections devoted to each of the needs listed below.

- food
- water
- light
- air
- waste disposal
- environment

Include a brief description and correlation between the importance of each need and how it helps the creature live a long, healthy life. When students share their pamphlets with classmates, have them compare and give examples of the ways living organisms depend on each other and their environments. Partner students and have them exchange pamphlets. Ask each student to evaluate his or her partner's pamphlet based on the criteria below.

- images/visuals
- clarity of text
- accuracy of ideas
- information/facts provided

Display the pamphlets in the school library or on a special bulletin board!

Name _____ Date _____

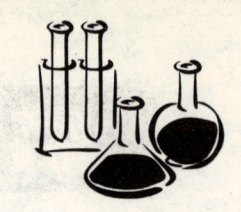

Science Snippets

Brainstorm

Write seven sentences from the reading that best describe what it was about.

_____
_____
_____
_____
_____
_____
_____

Underline or highlight the words and phrases you would like to use for your poem. Choose the words and phrases that best describe the topic.

Poem

Write the first draft of your poem using only the words and phrases you highlighted above.

_____
_____
_____
_____
_____

43 Planetary Exploration

Select books about our solar system to read aloud. Demonstrate how to assimilate new information with previously learned concepts by pausing to think aloud and ask questions at various points in the reading. Display books in the classroom about early space exploration and astronomers. After reading several sources, make charts or tables comparing facts about the planets. Students can use these charts to summarize their readings either in small groups or in their science journals.

Books About Space
Astronauts (Rookie Read-About Science: Space Science) by Carmen Bredeson
Max Goes to the Moon: A Science Adventure with Max the Dog by Jeffrey Bennett
Mission to Mars by Franklyn M. Branley
The Planets in Our Solar System (Let's Read-and-Find Out Science, Stage 2) by Franklyn Branley
There's No Place Like Space: All About Our Solar System by Tish Rabe

44 Building Your Case

Predictions are an important part of reading in any subject area. Help students practice making predictions based on the evidence presented in texts.

After reading a selection, ask students to make a prediction about something related to the topic. For example, after reading about the water cycle, predict what will happen after a flood. Instruct students to reference specific evidence in the text to support their predictions.

Make a photocopy of "Making Predictions" on page 52 for each student, and model how to use the reproducible. Write a prediction on the landing of the staircase. Then describe how you arrived at the prediction or what lead to the landing. Insert the supporting evidence on the stairs that lead to the landing. Tell students that the evidence on the stairs supports the prediction!

Prompt students to make their own predictions using the reproducible.

© McGraw-Hill Children's Publishing — 0-7424-2698-X *Every Teacher Is a Reading Teacher: 101 Ways to Incorporate Reading into Your Classroom*

Name _____ Date _____

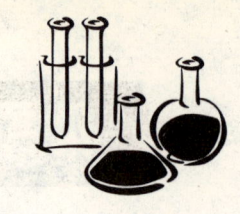

Making Predictions

Make a prediction based on evidence from the reading. Write the evidence on the stairs and your prediction on the landing.

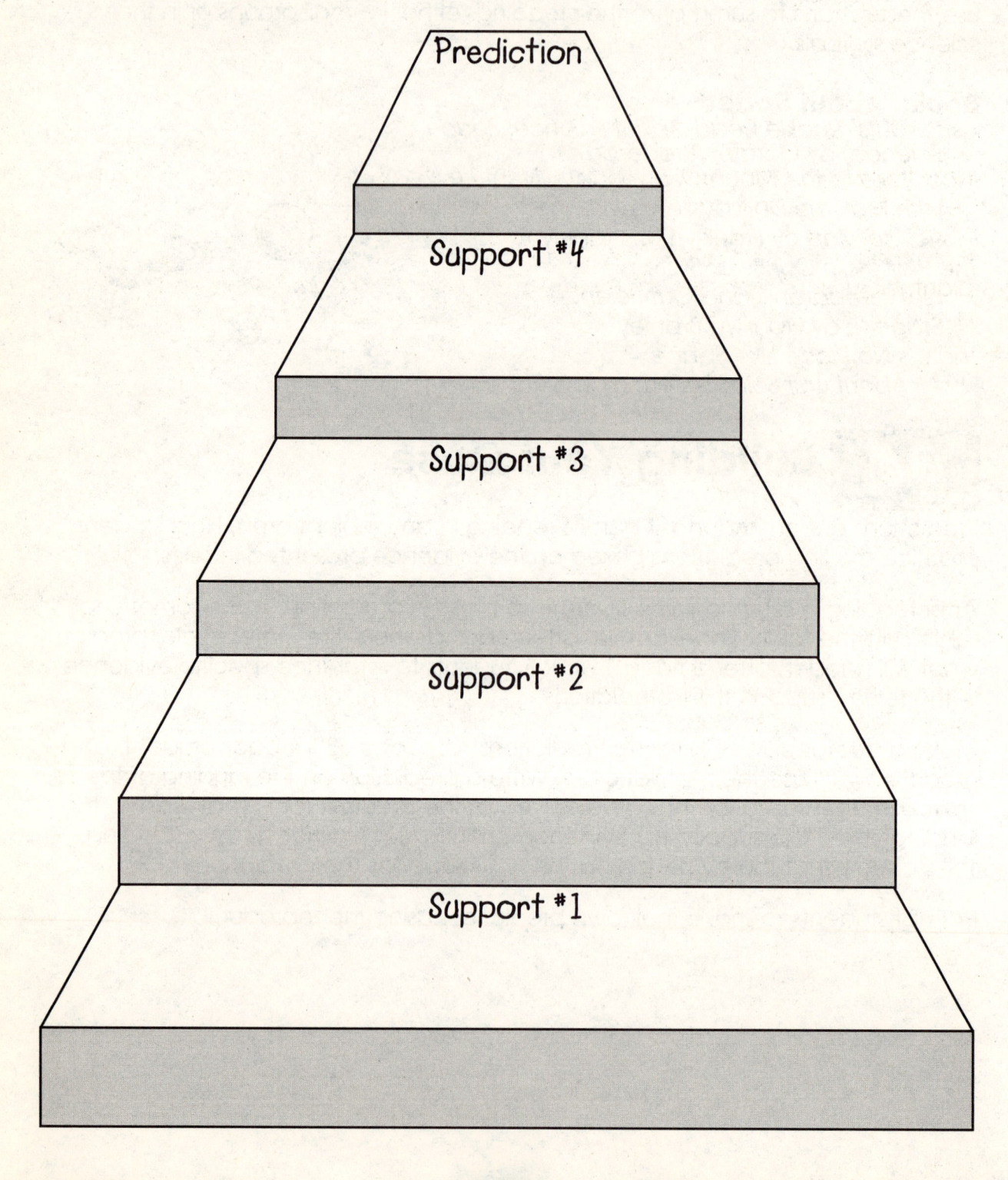

Prediction

Support #4

Support #3

Support #2

Support #1

45   **A System of Parts**

Gather a variety of reading materials on plants and animals for students to use in small groups. The material should include the identification and functions of plant and animal parts.

Study and identify parts of systems necessary for an organism's survival. Discuss the similarities and differences between the functions of plant parts and animal parts. Construct a Venn diagram or T-chart to record these answers, and have group members share their findings with the class. Refer to the reading material to support your findings.

Extend this idea during a unit on plants. Discuss how individual parts function to help the whole plant survive. Read about the stems, leaves, roots, and flowers. Set aside a bulletin board for students to create a large display.

From their readings, have students identify, draw, and label each part of a plant. Include an enlarged complete plant with string connecting each part to a card with facts and learned information. Review the material several times during the unit. Have different students read the cards aloud and explain the plant parts to the class.

While reading about plants and animals, have students complete the "Discovering the Main Idea" reproducible on page 54 for a paragraph in the text. Select a paragraph in the text, and ask students to determine the main idea. Instruct them to write the main idea in the box at the top of the page. Then have students find details in the paragraph that support the main idea and write them in the designated boxes.

Have students complete the organizer individually for a single paragraph. As an alternative, assign a different paragraph to each student. Make sure students share their findings while the rest of the class listens.

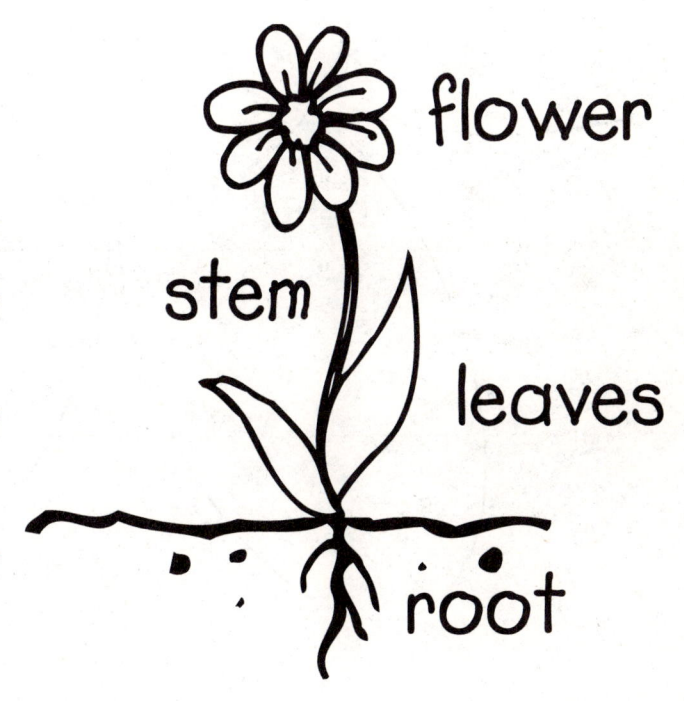

Name _____ Date _____

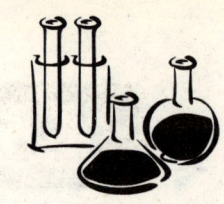

Discovering the Main Idea

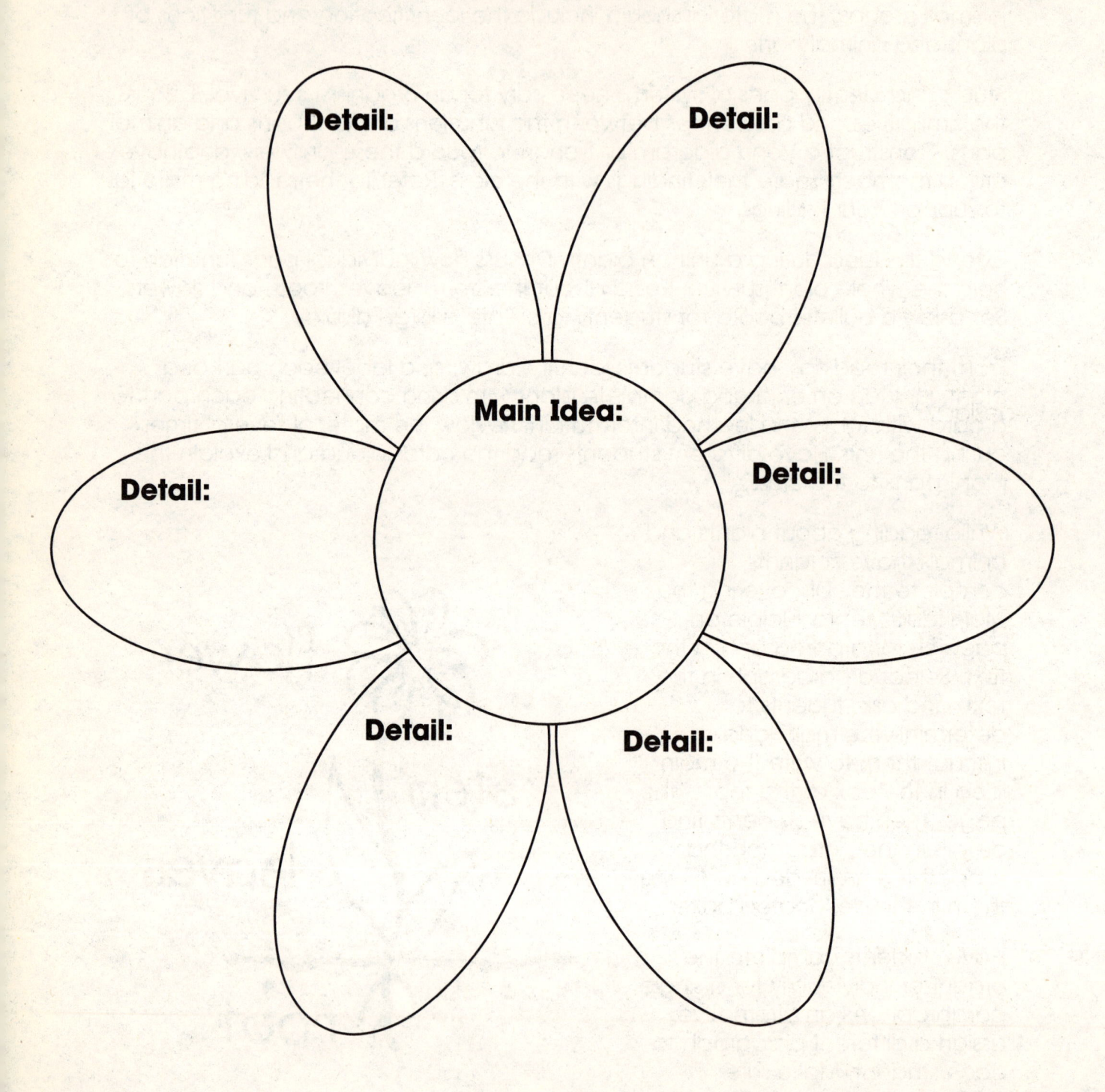

Detail:

Detail:

Detail:

Main Idea:

Detail:

Detail:

Detail:

46 Surfing for Science

Instruct students to explore simple machines using simple nonfiction books and the Internet. Find articles explaining what simple machines are and how they work. Demonstrate how to find answers to science questions on the Internet by navigating children's Web sites such as Yahooligans, Ask Jeeves for Kids, AOL Netfind for Kids, and KidsClick! Help students read to find the answers to the questions below.

- What is a simple machine?
- What are the six classes of simple machines?
- Describe each class and give an example.
- Explore several Web sites to compare articles. Which site is most helpful to you?

Based on their research, students can focus on one simple machine and then design a commercial or marketing campaign to sell it to their classmates. Review advertising strategies with students including the elements of persuasive writing. Remind students to remember their audience. Have students include posters or eye-catching pamphlets to explain what makes their simple machines so important. Display finished products in a common area to share with other classrooms.

47 Healthy Snacks

During a unit on nutrition, discuss why it is important to make healthy eating choices. With students, brainstorm reasons for eating well and how choosing poorly can affect the body. Find books and magazine articles on nutrition that give examples of well-balanced meals, and have students keep a journal of the food they eat for a week. Share journal entries at the end of the exercise and review nutritional facts learned from the readings.

Instruct students to bring in the packages or wrappings from three of their favorite snacks. Have them read the nutrition labels and complete the "A Study in Snacks" reproducible on page 56. Students will compare the contents of three snacks and decide which one is the healthiest choice. Post students' completed activity sheets, so classmates can compare labels.

Discuss the role marketing plays in getting someone to purchase certain snacks. What words or sayings do you see on food packaging and wrappers that encourage people to buy that product? Are some of the ingredients highlighted more than others? How does that help sales for that snack? What can we do to make sure we make healthy snack choices?

Name _____ Date _____

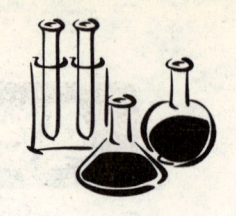

A Study in Snacks

Bring in the nutrition labels from three of your favorite snack foods. Examine and compare the nutritional content. Complete the chart below for each snack to see which one is the healthiest. Compare your findings with your classmates' findings.

	Snack 1	**Snack 2**	**Snack 3**
Brand name of snack			
Serving size			
Calories			
Total fat			
Sodium			
Potassium			
Total carbohydrates			
Sugars			
Protein			
Vitamin A			
Vitamin C			
Calcium			
Iron			
Vitamin D			

Which of your snacks is the healthiest for you? Explain.

_____
_____
_____
_____

© McGraw-Hill Children's Publishing

0-7424-2698-X *Every Teacher Is a Reading Teacher: 101 Ways to Incorporate Reading into Your Classroom*

48 Changing Shape

Read books on weathering and how forces in nature shape Earth's surface. Create a display or bulletin board with various landscapes and a related question for each picture. Invite students to explore and investigate to find the answers. Demonstrate how to use children's Web sites, such as Ask Jeeves for Kids, Yahooligans, Web Weather for Kids, Exploratorium, and The Curriculum Archive, to conduct research. Through their reading, challenge students to create their own questions to add to the board.

Example:

Sand Dunes: How were these piles of sand formed?

Grand Canyon: How has this wonder changed through the years and why?

Rivers: How do rivers change Earth's surface?

Glaciers: What happens to the ground when "rivers of ice" flow down a mountain?

Rain: How have floods and heavy rainfall changed Earth?

Further your students' knowledge of Earth's surface by doing a unit on weather. During the unit, ask students to brainstorm and list reasons why it is necessary to forecast wisely. Some possible answers may include: *So people can be prepared for storms and dangerous situations; So you can dress appropriately and plan your day; So farmers can organize their planting schedules.*

Discuss wild and unpredictable storms and the effects they have on people's lives, as well as Earth's surface. Gather books from the library that illustrate and explain wild weather. Invite students to research blizzards, floods, lightning, tornadoes, and hurricanes. Then have them write a summary of each type of major storm based on their readings.

Books About Weather

Extraordinary Wild Weather by Paul Dowswell

Wild Weather: Blizzards! by Lorraine Jean Hopping

Wild Weather: Drought by Catherine Chambers

Wild Weather: Floods! by Lorraine Jean Hopping

Wild Weather: Soup by Caroline Formby

Wild Weather: Thunderstorm by Catherine Chambers

Wild Weather: Tornadoes! by Lorraine Jean Hopping

49 Earth Fieldtrips

Read Joanna Cole's *The Magic School Bus Inside the Earth* as a whole group. Discuss and draw visual images based on the text's descriptions. Break the story into acts and build sets or props for a dramatization of the book. Have students reread the text and choose parts. Several students can take turns acting out the same parts. Encourage them to add to the story using facts they have researched and learned from other sources. Ask students to present their play to other classrooms or parents as a unit wrap-up.

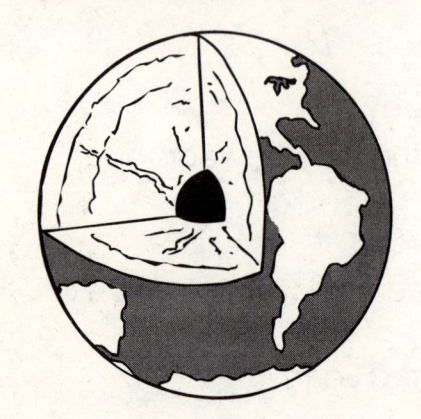

Extend student learning by researching different processes that take place on Earth. For example, explore the properties of water and the water cycle through a raindrop's perspective. First, gather fiction and nonfiction books on water and the water cycle. Have students read in small groups to become familiar with new terminology. Next, explore each stage of the cycle with students using illustrations and descriptions. Discuss chronological order from several starting points.

When students are comfortable with the process, invite them to see the cycle as if they are raindrops. Invite students (or "raindrops") to write diary entries of their experiences as they journey through each part of the water cycle. Have them use correct science terminology, and have students vary where they begin their voyages. Have them illustrate each diary entry and display their finished products.

Use the "A Raindrop's Diary" reproducible on page 59 for students to record their diary entries. Remind them to illustrate each stage of their journeys.

Books About Our Earth

The Magic School Bus at the Waterworks by Joanna Cole
Splish Splash by Joan Bransfield Graham
Water Dance by Thomas Locker
The Water's Journey by Eleonore Schmid

Name _____ Date _____

A Raindrop's Diary

On today's journey, I:

_____

_____

_____

_____

_____

_____

_____

_____

_____

_____

© McGraw-Hill Children's Publishing

0-7424-2698-X *Every Teacher Is a Reading Teacher:*
101 Ways to Incorporate Reading into Your Classroom

50 The Recycling Gazette

Read about and research conservation and the benefits of recycling. Send students on a mission in the school library to find as many materials on this topic as they can. Encourage a wide array of print, such as fiction, nonfiction, Internet articles, magazines, journals, newspapers, poems, and so on. Pool students' findings back in the classroom to compare and contrast the information provided in each source.

Based on their readings and discussions, create a classroom recycling newspaper. Begin by letting students peruse several local newspapers to see how information is formatted, such as the headlines, captions, pictures, facts, credits, and advertisements. Point out that the most important information always comes at the beginning of an article. Then ask students to submit several pieces for publication. Incorporate informational summaries, student poems, polls and surveys they've conducted with their schoolmates, and graphics created from their research.

Display the classroom newspaper in a common area of the school or library, and advertise the final product. Have students come up with persuasive ways to get their schoolmates to read their newspaper.

51 Calling All Astronomers!

Explore space from the comfort of your classroom. Log on to several astronomy Web sites and delve into facts and activities about the solar system and our universe. This is a great way for students to discover how reading can help them find information. You may want to brainstorm with students a list of key words, such as *astronomy, astronauts, space exploration, solar system, planets,* and so on, to help them learn how to do an effective Internet search.

Make copies of the "Calling All Astronomers!" reproducible on page 61 for students to help them navigate the Internet. Encourage them to learn what it takes to become an astronaut. They can research particular points of interest, play space games, and learn about the latest scientific discoveries. After students complete their space explorations, have them share their research with the class.

Name _____ Date _____

Calling All Astronomers!

Log on to an astronomy Web site to begin your space exploration. Your mission has four parts. You must complete each section and return to Earth safely. Good luck!

Part 1: Fact Finding

Write facts that are new and interesting to you about space and the solar system. Tell why they are interesting to you.

_____

_____

Part 2: Games and Activities

During your exploration, did you find any fun space games or activities? Write which games and Web sites you think are the best, and explain why others should try them.

_____

_____

Part 3: Glossary

Write three science terms that are new to you. Use the dictionary or your science glossary to find the meanings. Write the terms and their definitions.

_____

_____

_____

Part 4: Questions

Write three questions based on your knowledge of space. Challenge your fellow explorers to use Web sites to find the answers.

_____

_____

_____

© McGraw-Hill Children's Publishing   0-7424-2698-X Every Teacher Is a Reading Teacher:
101 Ways to Incorporate Reading into Your Classroom

52. Writing About Weather

Collect two storybooks with a science theme for practice in fluency and reading skills. For example, use *Cloudy with a Chance of Meatballs* by Judi Barrett and *Farmer Joe's Hot Day* by Nancy Wilcox Richards to coordinate with a weather unit.

Read the stories several times and practice different skills each time. Some skills are listed below.

- Compare the stories with other books or a personal experience.
- Tell the problem in each story and how it was solved.
- Draw the setting, the main character(s), or a favorite event from the story.
- Look for and write words with the same spelling patterns.
- Make a timeline for each story and compare them.

Next, ask students to write their own weather-related storybooks. Brainstorm ideas with students, and then have them write, edit, illustrate, and publish weather stories. Encourage students to read their finished books to an audience.

53. Beings with Backbones

Search the library or Internet for materials on animals with vertebrae. Include fiction and nonfiction selections. Group the books or articles into those about mammals, reptiles, birds, amphibians, and fish. Discuss the similarities and differences between the animals in the groups.

Copy the "Vertebrates Web" reproducible on page 63 for each student. Lead them in completing the activity sheet. Point out that outlines, webs, and diagrams make information easy to record and remember, and they can also be used as tool for organizing information for a report or research project. Have students begin by dividing vertebrates into the five main groups. In the smaller circles, they should provide examples from each group.

Help students use the map and information from the reading to create diagrams labeling each group's general body structure. Instruct students to record facts explaining how each animal meets its basic needs. Use the diagrams to create a bulletin board where students can keep adding information on vertebrates as they continue to study and learn.

Name _____ Date _____

Vertebrates Web

A vertebrate is an animal that has a backbone or spine. Vertebrates are categorized into five main groups. Use the categories in the box to label the web. In the smaller ovals, write examples of animals found in that group.

| Fish   Birds   Reptiles   Mammals   Amphibians |

Vertebrates

54 Fuel for the Body

Discuss how every human action requires energy that comes from food. Brainstorm with students the ways the body signals that it needs more food or that it is full. Have them read about and research the basic food groups and good nutrition. Instruct students to complete "The Food Pyramid" reproducible on page 65. Ask students to label each group with its name and the amount of recommended daily servings.

From your readings, construct a class food pyramid on a bulletin board. Have students search for examples in each group. Use encyclopedias, books, magazines, the Internet, and disposable items or clean food wrappers brought from home to decorate each part of the food pyramid with appropriate foods.

Demonstrate for students how to take notes on a particular text passage. First, have them read the passage or article for the main idea. Then, reread to select a few sentences that best represent the overall point of the paragraph or passage. Write these sentences in a science journal or notebook. When finished with the entire passage, discuss and compare the sentences chosen for the main ideas.

Students can refer to these notes as a review for a unit wrap-up. They can also use them to formulate questions to ask their classmates in preparation for a test or other assessment.

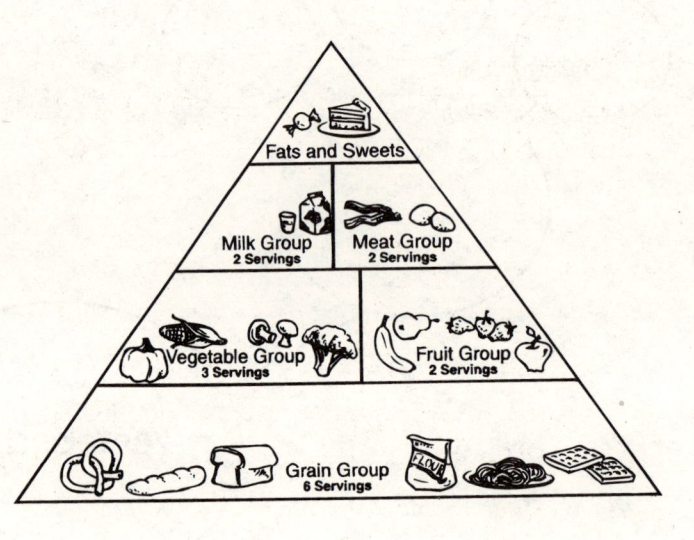

55 Good Vibrations

Try to find multiple copies of Joanna Cole's *The Magic School Bus in the Haunted Museum: A Book About Sound* to read in small groups. Focus on new vocabulary. Model how to use the characters' dialogue and the informational bubbles to figure out unfamiliar words. Study the affixes and create a vocabulary list for the book.

Discuss how vibrations are heard and how they travel through different media. Draw and discuss visual images based on the text descriptions. If possible, watch the video of this story, and use a Venn diagram to compare and contrast the two versions.

Name _____ Date _____

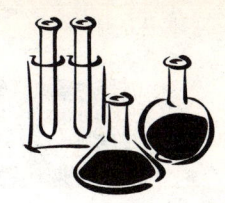

The Food Pyramid

Inside each part of the food pyramid, include the following.

- The name of the basic food group.
- The number of recommended servings per day.
- Examples of foods in each group.

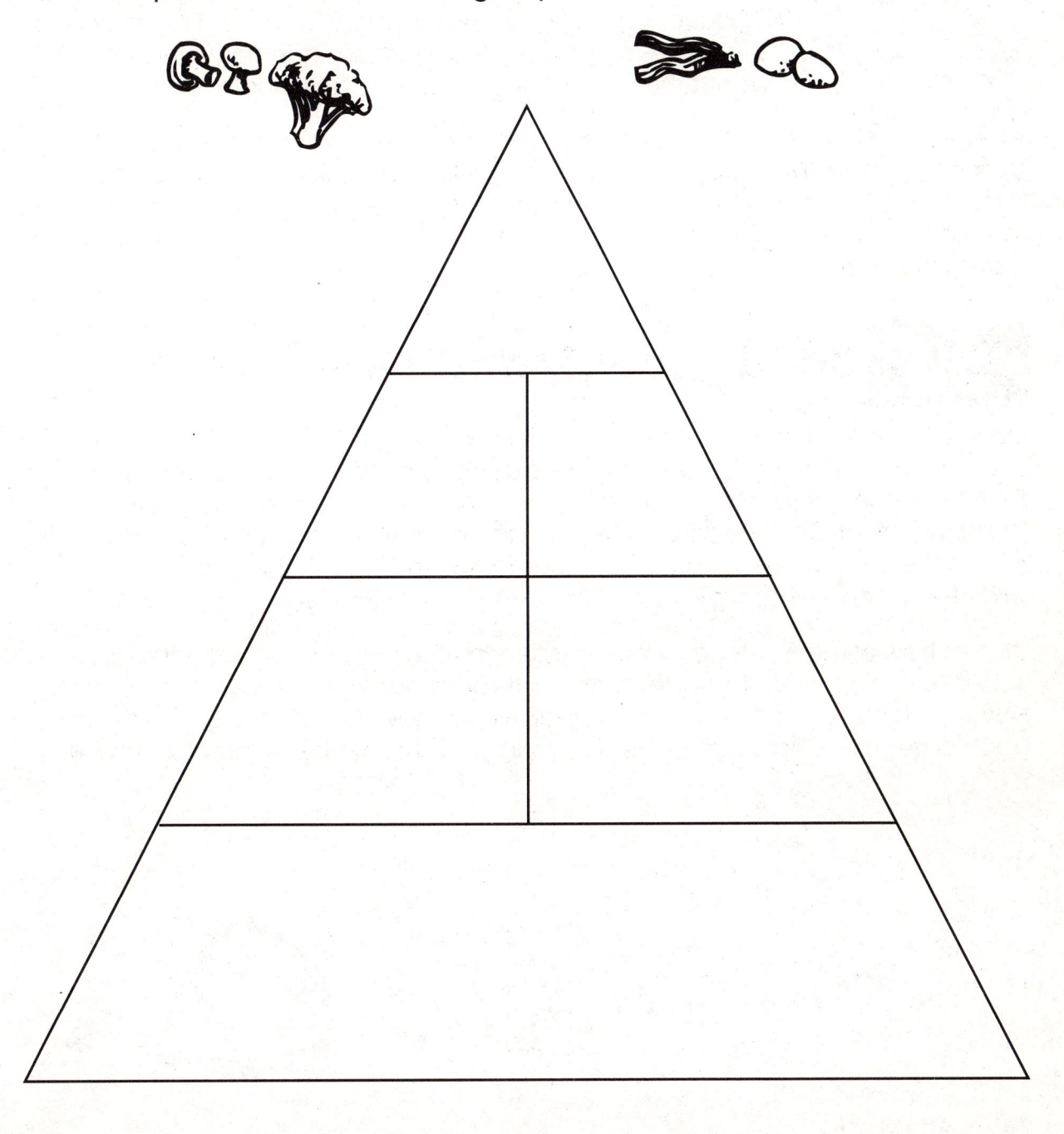

56 Tools of the Trade

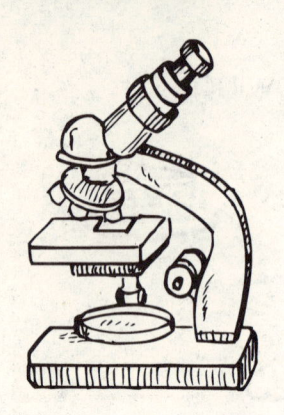

Display a variety of tools and methods to conduct science inquiry, such as a microscope, hand lens, ruler, balance, magnet, and compass. Introduce scientific tools using the KWL method.

Make a three-column chart on large print or butcher paper. Title the first column *What We Already Know*. Ask students to brainstorm and list the facts they already know about each tool and its uses. Title the second column *What We Want to Know*. Write down any questions students have about these instruments prior to the lesson or unit.

As they read books or other sources, students can record learned facts in their science journals. Wrap up the unit by completing the third column together, *What We Learned*. Analyze the chart and review the answers to the questions in the second column. Students can use their journal entries as notes to help them with the review.

57 Solid, Liquid, and Gas

Identify the three forms of matter—solid, liquid, and gas. Discuss the characteristics of each form, and ask students to draw examples based on your descriptions. Then have them research various forms of matter in their environment. Copy the "Solid, Liquid, or Gas?" reproducible on page 67 for each student. Have students search their environment and study these forms. Encourage them to correlate what they see to what they read.

Discuss how some matter can be classified in more than one category. Use water as an example that can fit into all three groups (rain, snow, and steam). Have students take notes in their journals about how water changes to fit into each category. Challenge students to find and share other examples as well.

Name _____ Date _____

Solid, Liquid, or Gas?

Read and collect information about solids, liquids, and gases. As you research, write examples of each form in the columns below. Think about your daily routine and the environment you live in to try to find as many examples as you can.

Solids	Liquids	Gases

Think About It!

Which items listed above belong in more than one column?
_____
_____
_____

Which items listed above belong in all three columns?
_____
_____
_____

58 Unusual Animals

Invite students to explore unusual animals and their habitats. Have each student choose an animal to research. Students can collect information from books, magazines, encyclopedias, and the Internet. Have them write six to ten interesting facts about the animal, as well as study the native region where the animal is found and locate it on a map. Ask students to draw a picture of their animal's environment and describe how the animal meets its basic needs. Remind students to read for the most interesting and unusual information. For example ask: "Does the animal have unusual sleeping habits? Does it eat strange things? Can it change colors or use camouflage? What does it do in the winter to stay warm if it lives in a cold climate?"

When they are finished with their research, invite students to share their animal research with the class. Encourage them to explain why they chose their animals.

Examples:

ermine	porcupine	dingo
orca	chevrotain	dugong
ostrich	gibbon	echidna
pronghorn	sloth	platypus
lemming	chinchilla	toucan

59 Science in the Spotlight

Have student research careers in science using the Internet, library, and community resources. They can do this individually or in small groups. Collect autobiographies, biographies, and other materials on a wide array of science careers. If possible, invite local volunteers from different science-oriented professions to talk with students about their jobs and career paths. Remind students that reading for information is one of the best ways to learn, and that they will do it throughout their lives.

Using their research, students can share information in a variety of formats. For example, they might: dress in career attire and take questions from the class as a member of their chosen profession; present an informational overview of the job; choose an important figure from the selected field, display a timeline of his or her accomplishments, and describe the allure of this career.

60 Science and Literature

Explore the built-in connection between science and literature in science fiction. Begin by teaching students about the genre. Science fiction includes some or all of the elements listed below.

- Science
- Technology and invention
- The future and the remote past, including all time travel stories
- Scientific method
- Other places, like planets and dimensions, including alien visitors
- Catastrophes, natural or man-made

Read aloud from science fiction books appropriate for students' reading level. Take the opportunity to model appropriate pacing, inflection, and expression while reading. During the reading, pose questions about the feasibility of the inventions or concepts in the book. Read a few excerpts to stimulate interest, and have copies of the book available for students to read on their own.

61 On the Prowl

Study endangered animals with this fun guessing game. Divide the class into small groups. Hand each group a large index card with the name of an endangered animal printed on it. Send groups on a mission to collect information on their selected animal, including pictures of it in its natural habitat. Each group writes ten clues about its animal on the back of the index card. Make sure they include clues as to why the animal is endangered. Model how to take effective notes when researching, and then use notes to write clever, concise clues.

Post the names of all the endangered animals students studied. Have students share their clues while the rest of the class try to guess which animal is being described.

Endangered Animals

Aye-aye	Bald eagle	White rhinoceros
Bengal tiger	Black lemur	Barred owl
Giant anteater	Giant panda	Brown hyena
Indian cobra	Kit fox	Grizzly bear
Kodiak bear	Ocelot	Koala
Mountain gorilla	Polar bear	Okapi
Orangutan	Sloth bear	Sea otter
Spider monkey	Spotted bat	Snow leopard

SOCIAL STUDIES

62 Book Talks with Book Baskets

Hold book talks about social studies literature. Find picture books, stories, nonfiction and informative books, biographies, and historical fiction titles about history, geography, and economics. Ask each student to find a book about the topic the class is studying. It can be fiction or nonfiction. Allow students adequate time to read their books, and then announce a Book Talk. Each student shares briefly about the book he or she read. Model how to do the Book Talk by acting out the following steps.

- Show the book and read the title and author's name.
- Give a brief summary of the book, and highlight the main themes and important events in the plot.
- Finally, explain what you learned about the social studies topic by reading this book.

You may want to spend a few weeks modeling Book Talks, and then have students begin their own. Encourage students to follow your example and discuss the books they read. This activity usually inspires students to find other books about the same topic and read about it on their own! Place shared books in a special book basket. Students then have access to books of interest during reading time.

To help students find books for their Book Talks, display books in the classroom, provide a suggested reading list, or help students search the school library. Your school librarian is also a great resource. There are literally hundreds of titles related to social sciences. A suggestion list is given on page 72. For even more resources, consult one of several published bibliographies, or search the Internet for suggestions. Try the National Council for the Social Studies Web site for a list of Notable Social Studies Trade Books for Young People.

Suggested Titles for Social Studies

The age ranges and levels of these books vary. Use them according to students' needs, interests, and abilities.

Annie and the Old One by Miska Miles
Arrow to the Sun: A Pueblo Indian Tale by Gerald McDermott
The Ballot Box Battle by Emily Arnold McCully
A Boy Called Slow: The True Story of Sitting Bull by Joseph Bruchac
Buffalo Woman by Paul Goble
Corn Is Maize: The Gift of the Indians by Aliki
Crazy Horse's Vision by Joseph Bruchac
Dancing Teepees: Poems of American Indian Youth by Virginia Driving Hawk Sneve
Doctor Coyote: A Native American Aesop's Fables by John Bierhorst
The Eagle's Song: A Tale from the Pacific Northwest by Kristina Rodanas
Eyewitness: American Revolution by Stuart Murray
The Gift of the Sacred Dog by Paul Goble
The Girl Who Loved Wild Horses by Paul Goble
House Mouse, Senate Mouse by Peter W. Barnes and Cheryl S. Barnes
I Am Rosa Parks by Rosa Parks
I Have a Dream (Scholastic, 1997) by Martin Luther King, Jr.
If a Bus Could Talk: The Story of Rosa Parks by Faith Ringgold
Knots on a Counting Rope by Bill Martin Jr., et al.
The Legend of the Bluebonnet: an Old Tale of Texas by Tomie de Paola
The Legend of the Indian Paintbrush by Tomie de Paola
Let It Shine: Stories of Black Women Freedom Fighters by Andrea Davis Pinkney
Marshall, the Courthouse Mouse: A Tail of the U.S. Supreme Court by Peter W. Barnes and Cheryl Shaw Barnes
More Than Anything Else by Marie Bradby
Native Americans Told Us So by Melvin Berger
Only Passing Through: The Story of Sojourner Truth by Anne Rockwell
A Picture Book of George Washington by David A. Adler
A Picture Book of Sacagawea by David A. Adler
Pocahontas, 1595–1617 by Liz Sonneborn
Sarah, Plain and Tall by Patricia MacLachlan
So, You Want to Be President? by Judith St. George
The Story of Johnny Appleseed by Aliki
Tapenum's Day: A Wampanoag Indian Boy in Pilgrim Times by Kate Waters
Through My Eyes by Ruby Bridges
The Warrior Maiden by Ellen Schecter
Washington's Birthday (Best Holiday Books) by Dennis Brindell Fradin
We Are the Many: A Picture Book of American Indians by Doreen Rappaport
We Were There, Too! Young People in U.S. History by Phillip Hoose
The Wigwam and the Longhouse by David Yue
Woodrow for President: A "Mice" Way to Learn About Voting, Campaigns, and Elections by Peter W. Barnes and Cheryl Shaw Barnes
Yonder Mountain: A Cherokee Legend by Robert H. Bushyhead, et al.
You Want Women to Vote, Lizzie Stanton? by Jean Fritz

63 Chart It!

One way to help students read and organize information is to create charts. You can make and photocopy charts for students, or ask students to create their own. There are many different kinds of charts, graphic organizers, and diagrams you can use to organize information.

Photocopy pages 74–76 for each student. Tell students that they can use these pages to practice reading and charting information. Model for students how to find and take notes from the reading by using the chart provided on page 76. You may want to make a large class chart for yourself that you can fill in as students follow along at their desks with their individual charts. Students begin by reading about the topic—the very first Americans. Then, they fill in the chart with facts noted during the reading. Encourage students to highlight important words, phrases, facts, and other information as they read. They can then easily find and copy this information in their charts. Remind students that charts and graphic organizers should be kept in a file for future reference. These are handy study tools for tests, unit reviews, and research papers.

64 The 5 Ws Reporter

This strategy helps students learn to become skillful, strategic readers and comprehend the most important information from their reading. It's very effective when studying government figures or famous people in history, such as presidents. This strategy can be used with a social studies textbook or some other type of literature about the topic. Tell students that this is a typical strategy used by newspaper reporters because they know this is one way readers will get the most important information about a person or event.

First, have students listen to or read a story about the famous person or government figure, such as a mayor, governor, or president. As they read, have them note the information that answers these questions—*who, what, when, where,* and *why*. Have students use "The 5 Ws Reporter" reproducible on page 77 to gather this information. After compiling these essential facts, invite students to write a short news article, making sure to answer the 5 Ws.

Display students' news articles on a bulletin board for others in your class or school to read. You can also design a classroom newspaper of all the articles, or conduct a newscast, giving each student the opportunity to read aloud his or her article as a reporter. Ask the class to evaluate if they effectively addressed the 5 Ws.

Name _____ Date _____

The Very First Americans

Many years ago, less people lived in America than now. The very first people to live in our country were the Native Americans. They lived all over the country in groups called *tribes*. The tribes were often quite different from one another. They lived in different kinds of homes, and some even spoke different languages. They were alike in one very special way. They all loved this land. They did their best to take care of the land and use only what they needed. Read about four of these tribes below.

Anasazi

The Anasazi tribe lived in the area we now call the state of Colorado. They built their homes in the cliffs. They used clay, stones, and mud to build their homes. The Anasazi grew their own food. They were farmers. They grew corn, squash, and beans. The children in the tribe did not have school, so they learned from the adults in their tribe.

Makah

Another tribe, the Makah, lived near the Pacific Ocean in the area we now call the state of Washington. There were many trees in this area, so the Makah built their homes using trees. They also built posts called *totem poles*. Totem poles were put at the openings of their homes and used as a doorway. Since the Makah lived near the ocean, fishing was important to them. They used canoes for fishing.

Name _____   Date _____

The Very First Americans (cont.)

Mohawk

The Mohawk lived in the area now known as the state of New York. There are many lakes and rivers in this area, so we know they used canoes to get around. They made their canoes from deerskin and trees. The Mohawk tribe lived in large homes called longhouses. Usually more than one family lived together in a longhouse. To get food, this tribe hunted, fished, and farmed.

Sioux

Another tribe was the Sioux. They lived in three areas of the United States now known as North Dakota, South Dakota, and Minnesota. This tribe moved around these states because they followed the buffalo. They hunted them using horses and bows and arrows. They needed them for food and to make their homes. They lived in homes made of buffalo skins called *tepees*. The Sioux were never wasteful. They used every part of the buffalo. They never killed more than they needed.

Name _____ Date _____

The Very First Americans Chart

Fill in the chart below with the information from your reading.

Tribe	Where They Lived	How They Got Food	Type of House	Transportation

Name _____ Date _____

The 5 Ws Reporter

1. **Who** am I reading about?
   _____

2. **What** is important about this person? What was the person's job or accomplishments?
   _____
   _____

3. **Where** did this person live or work? **Where** did this person do important things?
   _____
   _____

4. **When** did this person do these important things? **When** did they do their job or for how long?
   _____
   _____

5. **Why** is this person or the things he/she did important?
   _____
   _____

6. On the lines below, write a paragraph about the person you researched.
   _____
   _____
   _____
   _____

65 Preview Before You View!

The phrase "preview before you view" is a fun reminder to students to think and learn more about pre-reading strategies. Pre-reading strategies are important for every reader. Readers need a clear understanding of why they are reading. *What is the purpose for reading the material? What is the goal once finished?* If students have a clear understanding of these questions, their comprehension becomes more focused and successful.

Before reading, share the title or the main theme of the reading. For instance, if you are learning about maps, write the word *map* on the board. Ask students what they already know about maps and share their prior knowledge. Record their ideas on chart paper. Their ideas will give you a guide as to what you should focus on during the unit. Display a map of the world, your city, or state. This may generate more ideas from students who couldn't visualize the word *map* or may have limited English proficiency.

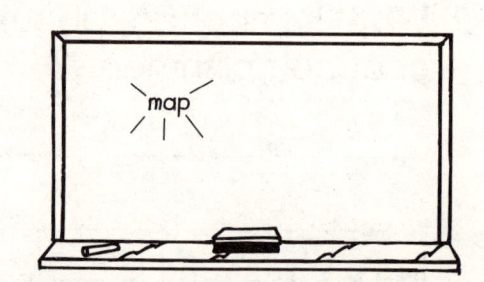

Next, show the book cover or the first page of the reading material. Have students look at the title and pictures and predict what they will be learning. Be sure to applaud all attempts in this discussion. There are no wrong answers here. Students are just making guesses.

Now, have students look at the pictures and illustrations with you. Pay special attention to headings and boldface or italicized words. Ask students why they think some text may be featured in this way. Explain that these are important words or ideas to know. Help them understand that the author wanted the words to stand out, so they were intentionally highlighted. Review vocabulary words that may be difficult for students. Take the opportunity to point out captions and labels for illustrations, photos, charts, and maps. Remind students that important information is almost always included here.

When you get to the end of the text, look for questions or notes from the author. These might come as a short chapter review or discussion questions. They may provide a clear understanding of what students should have learned from reading the material. Explain to students that they will need to know the answers to these questions when they are finished reading. If there are no questions at the end of the text, tell students your objectives and goals for the reading. List what you expect them to know and understand once they are finished. This will give them a purpose for reading!

"Preview Before You View!" on page 79 provides students with a handy checklist for previewing material. Tell them to use this checklist when previewing material on their own. It will help them to remember all the steps.

© McGraw-Hill Children's Publishing

Name _____ Date _____

Preview Before You View!

1. Think about and write what you already know about the topic.
   _____
   _____

2. Look at the title and write a prediction about the book or article.
   _____
   _____

3. Look through the text. Check the following boxes as you complete the list.

   ❑ Look for pictures.

   ❑ Look for bold/italic words.

   ❑ Look for captions/labels.

   ❑ Look for headings.

4. Check at the end of the reading for review questions. Write the questions below.
   _____
   _____

5. Write your purpose for reading.
   _____
   _____

6. Did you find the answers to these questions in your reading? Write the answers below.
   _____
   _____
   _____

66 Vocabulary Match-up!

Students will always have new vocabulary words to learn and understand. Use the following reading strategy throughout your social studies curriculum or any other subject. First, preview the material you are studying, or use your teacher's edition to search for words that may be difficult for students. This should be done before you read aloud to the class or before they read on their own. Share these words with your students as you complete pre-reading activities. For a review of pre-reading activities, see pages 78 and 79.

Go over the vocabulary words with the entire class or with small groups of students. Introduce each word and use decoding strategies to determine pronunciation. After decoding, decide on the meaning of the word. Use the word in a sentence, either from the text or your own, to determine meaning. This will encourage students to use context clues to determine meanings of unfamiliar words. Then, write the word and its definition, side by side, on chart paper. Next, have each student write the word on one index card and the definition of the word on another. Students should each have their own set of word/definition cards to take home as study tools for unit reviews, tests, and other assessments.

After the cards are finished, you are ready to play Vocabulary Match-up! This simple game is played similarly to the popular game *Concentration*. You may want to play this quick game before having students read the text. This develops fluency and understanding of new vocabulary while reading. Students will be less likely to get stuck on new words. This game also builds attention and memory skills.

| toy | a thing kids play with |

How to Play

1. Shuffle the cards and place them face down in rows.

2. The first player turns over two cards. If one is a word and the other is its correct definition, that player has a match. He or she keeps the cards and takes another turn.

3. If the cards do not make a match, the player turns over the cards again. The next player then takes a turn.

4. The goal is for players to try and remember where they have seen certain words and definitions, so they can make matches.

5. Once all the cards have been matched, players count their card pairs. The player with the most pairs wins!

67 Hamburger Order

Understanding order and sequence of events is often difficult for students in the earlier grades. Social studies concepts and topics usually include many historical events that require an understanding of beginning, middle, and end, as well as chronological dates.

One simple strategy for helping students understand sequencing is to relate it to something students already know. For example, most children have eaten a hamburger. Ask them to think about what they might like on a hamburger. Make a list of student responses on chart paper. Many will start with ketchup and then mustard, followed by lettuce, tomato, pickle, mayonnaise, and so on. Ask students to think of the order of events in the text like a hamburger! When you put a hamburger together, you start with the bottom bun. Then, you have the burger patty; next, your toppings; and finally, the top bun.

After reading social studies text that includes a clear sequence of events, such as the discovery of America, fill in the "Build a Burger: Order of Events" reproducible on page 82 together with students. As students get better at understanding sequence of events, they will be able to complete the page independently. You may also modify the page to make your own hamburger with the appropriate number of toppings based on the number of events to be sequenced.

Name _____ Date _____

Build a Burger: Order of Events

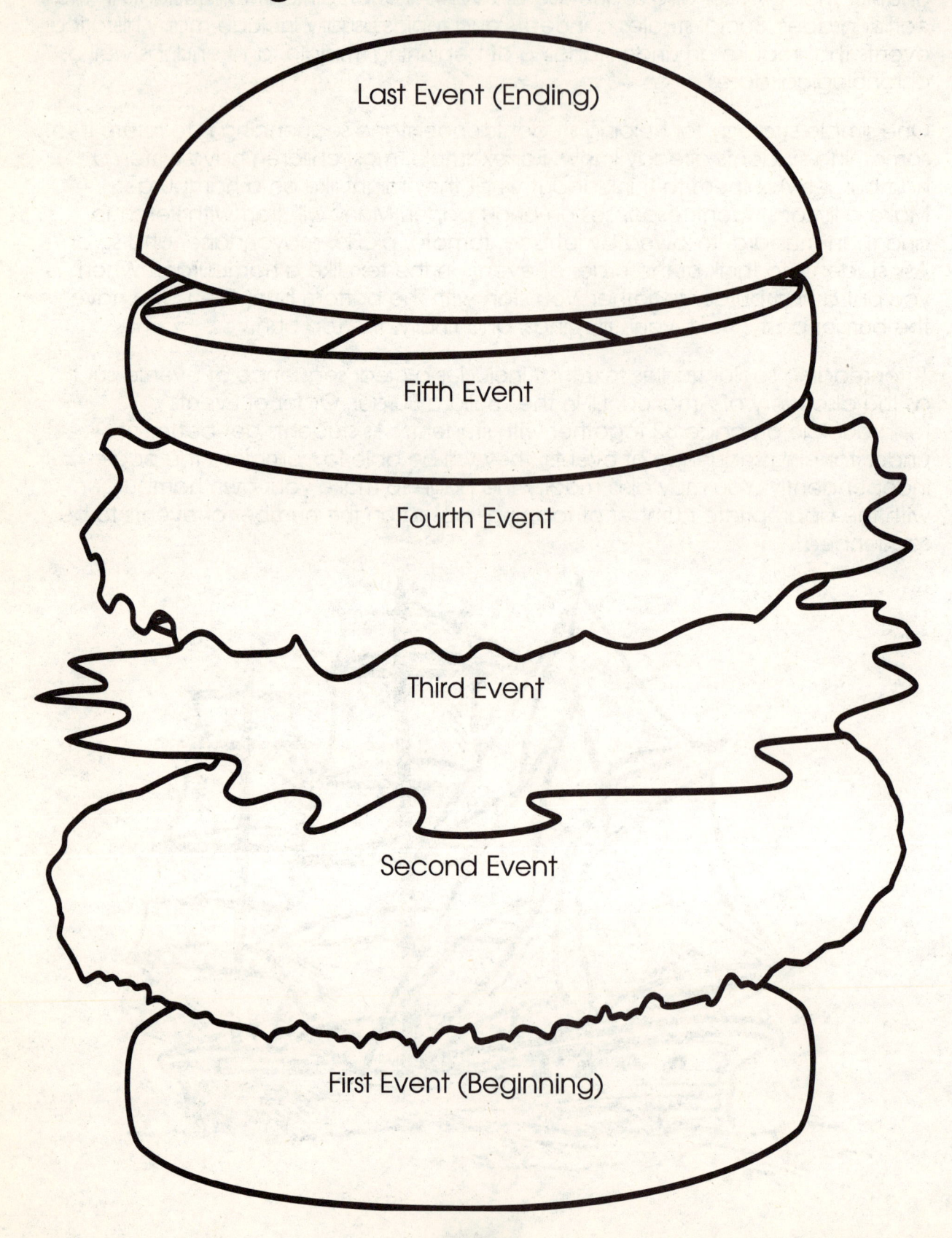

- Last Event (Ending)
- Fifth Event
- Fourth Event
- Third Event
- Second Event
- First Event (Beginning)

68 Community Comparisons

Learning about different communities is an interesting and important topic in social studies. The similarities and differences between the communities can be a little tricky. Students often get confused about what characteristics belong to each community. Most social studies texts discuss three basic types of communities—the city, suburbs, and farm or rural areas. The challenge is for students to understand each community and note the differences as well as similarities among them. Venn diagrams can be used as a quick and easy tool to compare and contrast any kind of topic or subject, including communities. See the Venn diagram below.

Begin your community study by making a copy of the "Community Comparisons: What Is a Community?" reproducible on page 84 for each student. Tell students to read the text and look for and highlight the unique characteristics of each community. Students may choose to use one color highlighter for noting unique characteristics and a different colored highlighter for noting similar characteristics.

When they are finished, have students complete the triple Venn diagram on page 85 to compare and contrast the three types of communities in the reading. Model for students how to work with a Venn diagram by writing unique characteristics for each community in the individual circles and similar characteristics in the intersecting areas of the circles.

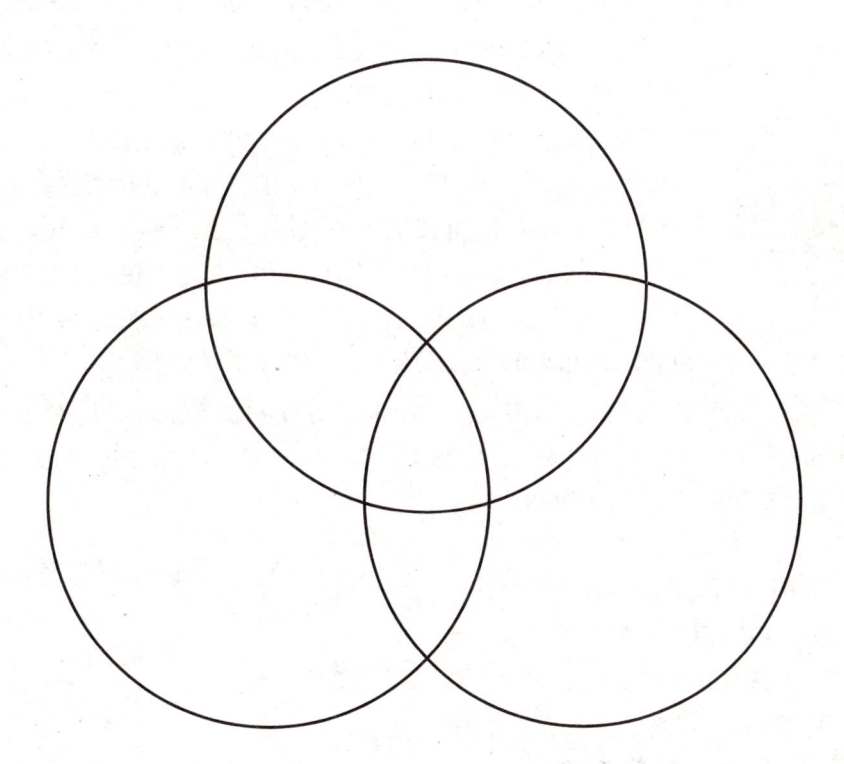

Name _____ Date _____

Community Comparisons: What Is a Community?

Read the following text about different kinds of communities.

A *community* is where people live. Most people like to live by other people, and so all types of communities have people. Communities are alike in several ways. Almost all communities have schools, stores, and homes where people live. There are three basic kinds of communities.

One kind of community is the *city*. A city is a big community. A lot of people live and work in the city. There are many things to do in the city. Cities have zoos, baseball stadiums, museums, malls, and apartment buildings. Many families can live in one building in different apartments. There are different kinds of jobs in the city, too. Some people work in office buildings, large factories, and stores. People from other kinds of communities may come into the city to work, even though they don't live there.

The *suburbs* are another kind of community. Suburbs are the areas right outside of a city. They are usually not as big as cities or as crowded. Most homes in the suburbs are houses, not apartments. People who work in the suburbs might work in smaller offices, schools, or stores. Some people live in the suburbs but work in the city.

The last kind of community is the *farm community*. Some people call this the *country* or *rural area*. This community usually has a lot of open space, animals, and trees. Many of the people who live here work and live on farms. They might grow vegetables or raise animals for food. Some people choose to live in the country because they enjoy the large, open spaces and the quiet.

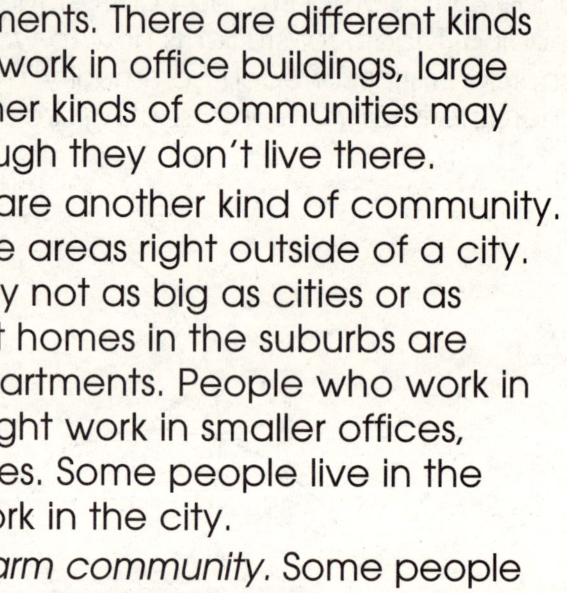

© McGraw-Hill Children's Publishing

84

0-7424-2698-X *Every Teacher Is a Reading Teacher: 101 Ways to Incorporate Reading into Your Classroom*

Name _____ Date _____

Community Comparisons: Venn Diagram

Think about the communities in your reading. Compare and contrast them in the triple Venn diagram below.

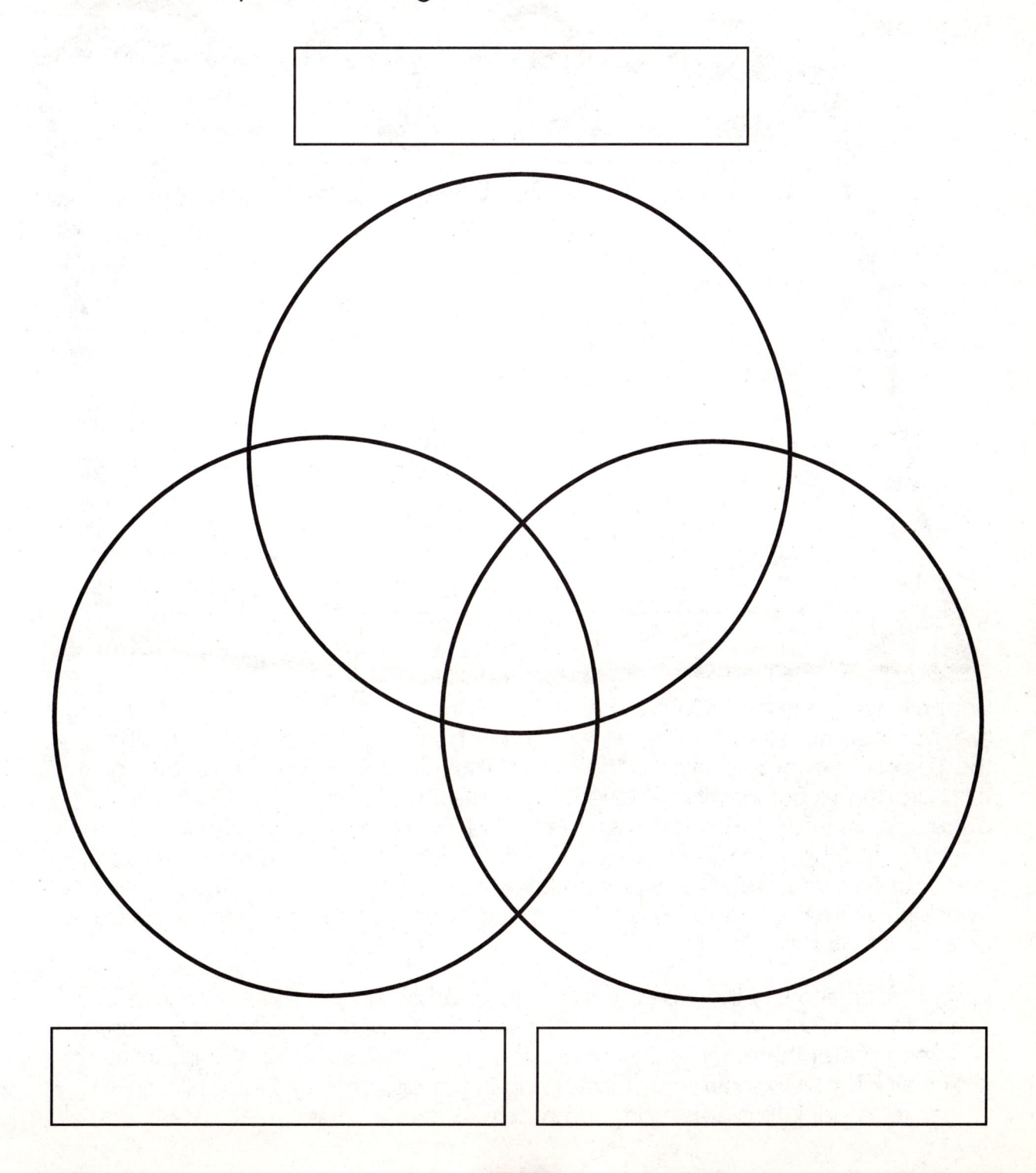

69 Class Communities Chart

After having students complete the Venn diagram on page 85, make a class chart showing the different types of jobs, services, buildings, and so on, one would find in different communities. Make a large chart on chart paper or the board, and have students think of examples based on their reading and what they learned from filling out the Venn diagram.

Example:

Cities	Suburbs	Farm Community
tall buildings	library	barns
hospital	houses	farms
parks	parks	large, open spaces
apartment buildings	schools	trees, animals

Finally, have students choose the type of community in which they would like to live. Ask them to explain, in detail, why they chose that community and why they prefer its characteristics to the others. This may be difficult for second and third graders to put in writing. Have them share this verbally in a classroom discussion, as you list their ideas on the board. For advanced students, you could try another triple Venn diagram. Write students' words as they say them. Point out that you are writing their exact words. They will see how their ideas are transferred into print. Help children read and understand each word or phrase as you write it.

Invite students to use the words in the class chart to write a short paragraph about their favorite kind of community. They should write or dictate the reasons why they prefer this community rather than another. Ask students to illustrate their paragraphs to show themselves living in the community. Bind children's pages together into a classroom community book!

70 Famous American Riddles

Children usually enjoy reading and studying about the presidents of the United States. They enjoy learning interesting facts and trivia, especially stories or legends about the presidents' childhoods. For example: George Washington and the cherry tree, and Abraham Lincoln teaching himself to read by firelight. Researching famous people of interest is a great way to get even the most reluctant readers involved!

Ask each student to choose a president he or she is interested in learning more about. Don't worry if two children are interested in the same president. They usually come up with completely different facts about the same person. Encourage students to use a variety of sources to locate information about their presidents. They can use the school library, your classroom library, the Internet, or age-appropriate biographies. Have students record interesting facts on note cards. Encourage them to find at least five facts.

Then demonstrate how to write a riddle about someone famous. You may want to use your school principal. In the eyes of your students, he or she is pretty famous! Start with the most difficult clues first.

Example:

I go to school every day!
I have an office.
I help students learn.
I am in charge of the entire school.

Who Am I?

Help children create riddles about the presidents they researched. Read each student's riddle to the class. See how many clues it takes for students to guess each president. Display your class's riddles on a bulletin board or in a center. Index cards work well. You can write the riddle on one side and the answer on the other. Riddles are a wonderful tool for showing students how fun learning can be!

71 Personal Timelines

Timelines are often difficult for students to read and understand. Besides being an important aspect of social studies, timelines also challenge students to use their math and reading skills. Timelines include the concept of beginning, middle, and end, along with dates and sequential order. To help students comprehend social studies timelines, they first should understand timelines to which they can personally relate.

Start with a class timeline. Write it on the board or use chart paper. Your timeline should begin with the first day of school. Then, move into October and the celebration of Halloween. Next, there is conference time in November and the study of pilgrims and Thanksgiving. December follows with the holiday vacation and special parties. You could even personalize your timeline by adding students' birthdays and other important events that happened in your classroom. Next, ask students to think about what might happen in the future. What will you add to your timeline? Keep your timeline going throughout the rest of the school year. Construct it much like a number line with bullets and captions.

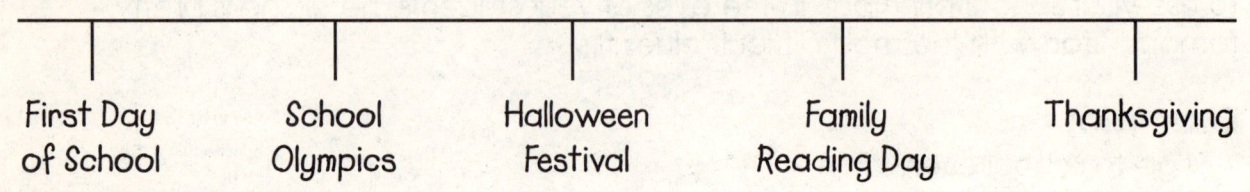

| First Day of School | School Olympics | Halloween Festival | Family Reading Day | Thanksgiving |

If you wish, construct your own personal timeline to share with students. Begin with the day you were born and continue through the present day. Highlight events like special celebrations and awards, family milestones, high school graduation, college, wedding, and the birth of children. Make sure to highlight the day you started teaching!

When students have a good understanding of the concept, invite them to construct their own personal timelines. Tell them they can include any special events, but that they should include the following.

- Their birth date
- When they learned to walk
- When they learned to talk
- When they lost their first tooth
- Their first day of school
- When they learned to read

Encourage students to work on their timelines at home. Have parents provide input about family and personal events. Invite students to decorate their timelines with pictures, drawings, and photos, and then share them with the class.

72 Word Scavenger Hunt

Children love scavenger hunts! For this engaging activity, give each student a piece of lined paper. At the top of the paper, have students write a word related to a current social studies topic being studied. Then have them draw vertical columns between each letter. Let them know that they will be going on a scavenger hunt for words! Have them look around the room and inside books for words that begin with the letter at the top of each column. Decide ahead of time how many words you want them to find for each column.

For example, if you are studying core democratic values and citizenship, have students write the word *liberty* at the top of their papers. Review the pronunciation and meaning of the word with students. Invite them to provide examples if possible. Then tell students to find other words that begin with the letters in the word *liberty*. As an extra challenge, encourage students to find words that have something to do with liberty. This will give them a better understanding of what the word means.

Pages 90 and 91 list the core democratic values and information about the Constitution. You may want to introduce students to word scavenger hunts using this information. Read aloud the information to students, and instruct them to highlight key words and phrases that begin with the appropriate letters. This material can be difficult for students at this grade level. Be sure to carefully review any unknown or key words and any new concepts. As you review the material, pause and ask students to give examples of these concepts from their real lives. For example: "What does it mean to be a good citizen? What does it mean to be equal? What is the freedom to 'pursue happiness'? What do you or your families do to 'pursue happiness'? Why do you think this is important?"

To reinforce these concepts, use literature such as *We the Kids: The Preamble to the Constitution of the United States* by David Catrow, *America Is . . .* by Louise Borden, and *America: A Patriotic Primer* by Lynne Cheney. These books may help you simplify what can be complicated topics for your students.

L	I	B	E	R	T	Y
life	individual	beliefs	equal	rights	truth	you
love	ideas	benefits	equality	religion	trust	yes
law	interests	branches	economic	representative	trade	your
legislative	institution	Bill of	elect	reason	triumph	
liberty	ideals	Rights	executive	rule	tolerance	
language	industry	balanced	express	race	tell	
license					talk	
limits					try	

Name _____ Date _____

Core Democratic Values

Life: A person's right to life cannot be violated except if your life or the lives of others is threatened.

Liberty: This includes personal freedom, political freedom, and economic freedom. This is the freedom for people to gather in groups. They can have their own beliefs, ideas, and opinions. People also have the right to express their opinions in public.

The Pursuit of Happiness: As long as you don't interfere with others, you have the right to seek happiness in your own way.

Common Good: This is working together for the welfare of the community or the benefit of all.

Justice: All people should be treated fairly in both the benefits and responsibilities of our free society. No individual or group should be favored over another person or group.

Equality: Everyone has the right to political, legal, social, and economic equality. Everyone has the right to the same treatment regardless of race, sex, religion, heritage, or economic status.

Diversity: The differences in culture, dress, language, heritage, and religion are not just tolerated, but celebrated.

Truth: The government and its people should not lie. The truth is expected on both sides.

Popular Sovereignty: The power of the government comes from the people. The people have authority over the government.

Patriotism: The people or citizens show a love and devotion for their country and its values. They can show this using words or actions.

Name _____ Date _____

The Constitution of the United States

Rule of Law: Both the people and the government must obey all laws.

Separation of Powers: The executive, legislative, and judicial branches of the government should be separate institutions, so no one branch has all of the power.

Representative Government: People have the right to elect others to represent them in the government.

Checks and Balances: The powers of the three branches of government—executive, legislative, and judicial—should be balanced. No one branch should be the most powerful. Each branch should have powers to check the actions of the other branches.

Individual Rights: Each individual has the fundamental right to life, liberty, economic freedom, and the pursuit of happiness. These rights are outlined in the Bill of Rights. The government should protect these rights and not place unreasonable restrictions upon them.

Freedom of Religion: The right to practice any or no religion without persecution or judgment by the government.

Federalism: The states and the federal government share power as outlined by the Constitution.

Civilian Control of the Military: The people control the military to preserve democracy.

73 Historical Fiction Mini-Books

Making mini-books is a great way for students to demonstrate their understanding of a story or concept. Most social studies topics can be supplemented and reinforced using historical fiction. This genre contains historical facts mixed with fictional accounts or even legends. These stories often contain a central theme or historical event and are sometimes written to provide the perspective of a specific time period or the people who lived then. These types of books are more advanced for the typical reader in second or third grade and should be presented as read-alouds. One way to reinforce comprehension, events, and characters is to have students create mini-books of the story.

Native American legends and stories are great for this activity. Begin by reading the story aloud. Then have students go back and retell the beginning, middle, and end of the story with their mini-books. The first page is the title and cover. The following page tells what happened first in the story. The next page tells what happened in the middle of the story or perhaps the problem. The last page tells what happened at the end of the story. On the back of the mini-book, students can illustrate and write about the their favorite part of the story.

Help students construct their mini-books by simply folding paper. Fold a sheet of paper into fourths. When you open the book completely or undo the folds, you have the inside. This is where students write and illustrate their favorite part of the story! See the example below.

Example:

My favorite part of the story was . . .

fold

_____
_____
_____
_____

_____
_____
_____
_____

Middle

Beginning

fold

End

Title Page

_____
_____
_____
_____

_____
_____
_____
_____

74 Family Traditions Interview

Learning about other cultures, countries, and traditions is a fascinating experience for young students. Children often believe that their own traditions are practiced by everyone else. They are intrigued and interested in learning about other cultures and traditions.

Use this opportunity to build on your students' reading, writing, and listening skills. Ask them to interview a parent or grandparent about a favorite family tradition. It might have to do with their heritage or just something special their family has adopted as a tradition. Before the interviews, make a class chart together and list different holidays, traditions, and customs. This will give students a better understanding of new vocabulary words before heading out to do interviews. Review good listening and interviewing skills with your students. Demonstrate how they should ask questions and then listen attentively to responses while taking notes.

Require students to read aloud the questions they will be asking during their interview. Allow them time to practice with partners. Let them know they can ask for help with spelling during their interviews, but that they must do the writing themselves. Students that need extra assistance with reading and writing may want to take along a tape recorder to tape their interviews.

Once students have completed their interviews, have them display what they learned for the class. Give them a variety of ideas. They could make a collage, write a short book, take pictures, or bring in items used for the custom or tradition. They might even bring in a special traditional food to share that goes along with the tradition. The possibilities are endless!

Have students use the "Family Traditions Interview Form" on page 95 to help them conduct their interviews. Encourage students to generate other questions they would like answered as well.

Name _____ Date _____

Family Traditions Interview Form

1. What is your favorite tradition or custom?
2. Why is it your favorite?
3. Is there any special food you eat? What?
4. Do you use costumes or decorations? Explain.
5. How long has your family practiced this?
6. Is there anything else you can tell me about it?

Name of Person

75 Navigating the National Anthem

Learning the national anthem has been a part of school curriculum. At sporting events and on special occasions, we hear our students singing its famous words. Students often have no idea what they are actually singing about. As educators, we need to help them to pronounce the difficult vocabulary and to understand the meaning of this important, inspiring song.

Begin by providing students with some background about the national anthem. Explain that the words were written by Francis Scott Key in 1814. Key had watched a battle at night between England and America. He was so overjoyed to see the American flag still flying the next morning that he wrote the words to the national anthem about the flag and the night's battle.

Next, write the words to the anthem on chart paper or sentence strips. Highlight the vocabulary words you want students to focus on, and display the sentence strips in a pocket chart. Begin by reading the title.

For example, ask students what they think the "star-spangled banner" really is. You may even have them close their eyes and visualize what a star-spangled banner might look like. Ask them to think of the definition of the word *banner*. Some students might suggest that a banner is a type of sign. Explain that *banner* is another word for *flag*. The author is referring to the American flag in this title. Our flag has stars on it, and Key refers to it as a "star-spangled banner."

Proceed by reading the anthem one line at a time. Help students to decode any new and unfamiliar words. Use the lyrics and questions on page 97 as a guide to reading the anthem with students. Have students highlight the underlined words as you read and discuss them.

After you finish teaching the meaning of "The Star-Spangled Banner," sing the song together. Music is an excellent way to reinforce reading skills! You may also want to read the book *The Star-Spangled Banner* illustrated by Peter Spier.

The Star-Spangled Banner

Read the lyrics and questions. Highlight the underlined words. Discuss the questions with your class.

Oh, say can you see, by the dawn's early light,

"What does the phrase *dawn's early light* mean?"

What so proudly we hailed at the twilight's last gleaming?

"What does *hailed* mean?" "What is the *twilight's last gleaming*?"

Whose broad stripes and bright stars, through the perilous fight,

"What does the word *perilous* mean?"
Look up this word in a dictionary.

O'er the ramparts we watched, were so gallantly streaming?

The word *o'er* is the short version of *over*.
"What are *ramparts*?" "What was gallantly streaming?" "What does the word *gallantly* mean?"

And the rockets' red glare, the bombs bursting in air,

"What is a *red glare*?"

Gave proof through the night that our flag was still there.

"What does *proof* mean?"

Oh, say, does that star-spangled banner yet wave

The term *yet wave* means "to still stand tall."

O'er the land of the free and the home of the brave?

"Who is the song referring to with the phrase *land of the free* and *home of the brave*?"

76 Understanding Maps

Maps can be very complicated reading for students. There is so much print scattered all over the place, students sometimes have a hard time making sense of it. One way for students to read and understand maps is take each piece of the map one step at a time. Students often don't know what to do with the map key. This element is essential for reading and comprehending everything on a map.

Begin by explaining the definition of a map. Ask, "What are maps for?" "Why do we use them?" "What do maps look like?" Explore students' prior knowledge about maps. Ask them to share if they've used maps before or have watched their parents use a map.

Next, show how a map is like a picture. If you have an aerial picture of a city and a map of the city, you might show how they are similar. Show students a simple map that has following features: symbols, a key, and directions. Explain the purpose of each feature.

As an extension, enlarge and copy the sample map below for students to examine. Go over each part of the map with your students. Point out different symbols, and explain that these stand for real things and places. Explain that the key contains symbols for the real places and things on the map. Finally, explain the direction words. Show the arrows that represent north, south, east and west. Post signs that represent these directions in your classroom.

Together, make a map of your classroom. Include symbols for things such as desks, chairs, and tables. Use a key to show what these symbols stand for. Show the directions on your map.

To extend students' understanding of maps, have them make a map of their bedrooms. Remind them to include symbols, a key, and directions. They can share their maps with the class.

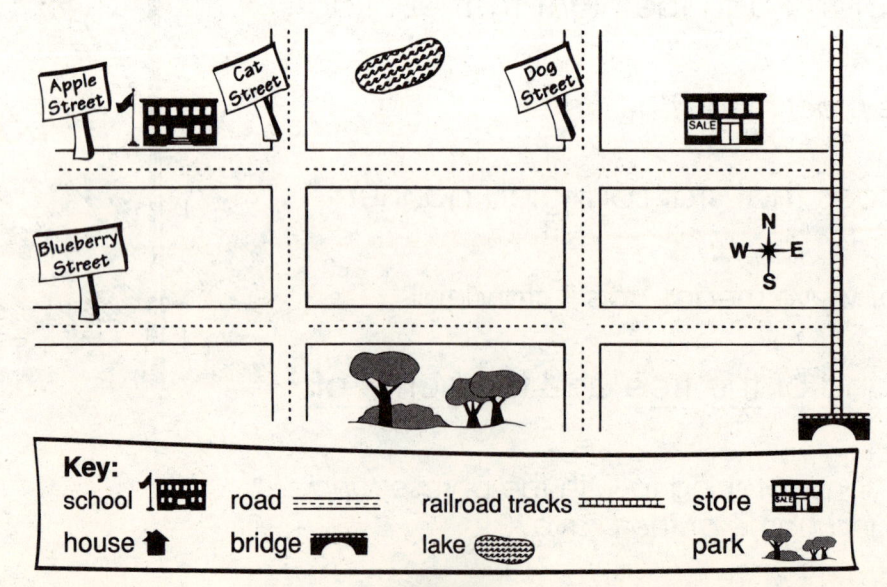

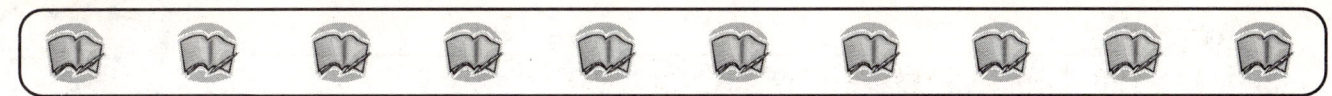

LANGUAGE ARTS

77 Reading Reflections

Keeping a record of the books they read allows students to analyze their progress, identify patterns in their reading habits, and recognize their accomplishments. Make several copies of the "Reading Reflections" reproducible on page 100 for each student. Place the pages in a file folder, large envelope, or small three-ring binder with the student's name on the front. This can serve as a reading log for the entire semester or school year. Each time a student finishes a book, ask him or her to record the information in their reading reflection log.

Sample Reading Reflection:

Title (Complete title):	Summary (Write a brief summary of the story.):	Personal Reflection (Explain your opinion of the book. Why did you like or dislike the book? Provide detailed reasons for your opinion.):
Miss Nelson Is Missing!	This book is about a nice teacher who has a terrible class. Her students are mean and nobody ever listens to her. So, . . .	I really liked this book! Miss Swamp was mean, and I didn't like her. I wouldn't want to be in her class. I thought . . .
Author (Who wrote the book?): Harry G. Allard		
Genre (What type of book is this? Fiction, biography, poetry, etc.): Fiction		

This collection of reading reflections can be a valuable resource for teachers as well as students. You can help students analyze their reading habits during a reader's workshop conference. Refer to the reading reflections to highlight the student's accomplishments during parent/teacher conferences. You may also consult these reflections when preparing to evaluate students' reading progress. Encourage students to share their writings with others when recommending books or starting discussions about a common book or theme.

Name _____ Date _____

Reading Reflections

Personal Reflection:

Summary:

Title:

Author:

Genre:

© McGraw-Hill Children's Publishing

0-7424-2698-X *Every Teacher Is a Reading Teacher: 101 Ways to Incorporate Reading into Your Classroom*

Suggested Titles for Language Arts

The age ranges and levels of these books vary. Use them according to students' needs, interests, and abilities.

A Is for Abigail: An Almanac of Amazing American Women by Lynne Cheney
Amber Brown Is Not a Crayon by Paula Danziger
Amelia Bedelia by Peggy Parish
The Boxcar Children Series by Gertrude Chandler Warner
Captain Underpants Series by Dav Pilkey
The Cat in the Hat by Dr. Seuss
Click, Clack, Moo: Cows That Type by Doreen Cronin
Cloudy with a Chance of Meatballs by Judith Barrett
Eloise by Kay Thompson
Frog and Toad Series by Arnold Lobel
Henry and Mudge Series by Cynthia Rylant
I'm a Manatee by John Lithgow
Junie B. Jones Series by Barbara Park
The Kissing Hand by Audrey Penn
Madeline Series by Ludwig Bemelmans
The Magic School Bus Series by Joanna Cole
Magic Tree House Series by Mary Pope Osborne
Math Curse by Jon Scieszka
Miss Nelson Is Missing! by Harry G. Allard
Officer Buckle and Gloria by Peggy Rathmann
Owl Moon by Jane Yolen
Ramona Quimby, Age 8 by Beverly Cleary
Ramona the Pest by Beverly Cleary
Stellaluna by Janell Cannon
Stone Fox by John Reynolds Gardiner
Strega Nona by Tomie de Paola
Sylvester and the Magic Pebble by William Steig
The True Story of the Three Little Pigs by Jon Scieszka

Poetry also appeals to many young readers. Explore some of the following titles:

The Giving Tree by Shel Silverstein
If I Were in Charge of the World and Other Worries: Poems for Children and Their Parents by Judith Viorst
A Light in the Attic by Shel Silverstein
The New Kid on the Block by Jack Prelutsky
The Stinky Cheese Man and Other Fairly Stupid Tales by Jon Scieszka
Where the Sidewalk Ends by Shel Silverstein

78 Fiction and Nonfiction

As students listen and respond to stories, help them learn to distinguish fiction from nonfiction. Read aloud a book such as Arnold Lobel's *Frog and Toad Are Friends*. Let students study the illustrations and tell if a picture shows something that could really happen or if it's made up. Tell them these are called picture clues. Picture clues can help students figure out what is happening in the text. Tell them this book is fiction. Explain that even though fiction books are made-up, they can also include events that could happen in real life.

Then read a nonfiction book about frogs and toads, such as *Frogs, Toads, and Turtles* by Diane L. Burns. This entertaining book is packed full of information for students to explore and investigate. Explain that a nonfiction book tells about facts. Discuss the facts of the book with students. Let them study the picture clues and explain what is happening, so they understand that the pictures show what can really happen. Display both books, and invite students to take turns telling how the two books are the same and different.

Next, have students work independently with fiction and nonfiction books. Ask them to choose two books on a similar topic, one that is fiction and one that is nonfiction. Encourage students to explore their books and complete a Venn diagram comparing and contrasting them.

79 Be a Bookworm!

Give students practice with identifying book titles, authors, and illustrators by having them record this information for the books they read. Copy the "Be a Bookworm!" reproducible on page 104 for each student. Have students cut out the bookworm head, write his or her name on it, and decorate it. Post the bookworm heads on the side of a wall or bulletin board. Whenever students finish reading a book, have them write the title, author, illustrator, and their personal rating on a body segment. Invite them to color and decorate the body segment and post it behind their bookworm's head. Watch as students' bookworms grow longer and longer! Invite students to take turns pointing out their favorite titles and telling why they liked the books.

80 Story Elements

After reading a book with students, help them learn to identify and describe the story elements. Photocopy the "Story Elements" graphic organizer on page 105 for each student. Instruct students to write the title, author, and illustrator of the book. Then have them describe the main characters, setting, plot, problem of the story, and solution. Finally, invite students to draw a picture of their favorite part of the story. Give each student an opportunity to share his or her descriptions and picture with the class. After doing this several times, students will be able to identify story elements quite quickly.

As an extension, encourage students to tell about the author's writing style and describe the illustrations. Were the illustrations realistic? Cartoon-like? Colorful? Was every part of the book illustrated, including the inside front and back covers? What kind of illustration was on the front cover? Were there photographs rather than illustrations? Tell students that illustrations can help them figure out difficult text.

Name _____ Date _____

Be a Bookworm!

Title: _____
Author: _____
Illustrator: _____
Your Rating: _____

Name _____

Name _____ Date _____

Story Elements

Title: _____
Author: _____
Illustrator: _____

Describe the story's main characters.

Describe the setting.

Describe the plot.

What is the problem?

What is the solution? (How did the characters solve the problem?)

On a separate sheet of paper, draw a picture of your favorite part of the story.

81 Book Re-cover-ing

As children read their favorite books, encourage them to describe the roles the authors and illustrators play in creating the texts. Copy the "Book Re-cover-ing" reproducible on page 107 for each student. After a student reads a book, have him or her write the title, author, illustrator. Ask them to copy and illustrate a favorite passage from the story or write a brief summary of his or her favorite part. Stress good penmanship by modeling how to write legibly, either in print or cursive. Explain that book covers are usually very colorful and attractive in order to grab readers' attention. They also provide clues about the story inside. Encourage students to consider these ideas as they create their book covers.

Give students a chance to present their finished products. Have them display both the actual cover and the created cover. Post a piece of butcher paper with the list below that students can refer to while presenting their books.

1. Read the title of your book.

2. Read the author's name.

3. Read the illustrator's name.

4. Describe your cover design for the book.

5. Talk about how the two covers are alike and different.

6. Read your favorite passage aloud to the class.

7. Explain why this is your favorite part of the book.

82 Morning Message

Each morning, have your students participate in a morning message by listening, reading, and speaking. Write your morning message on chart paper, and read it aloud. The message should state a welcome and name the day and date, as well as announce any special events like field trips, birthdays, assemblies, and projects. Use simple language with predictable words. You may even add some vocabulary words the class has been studying. Insert a few blank lines where these words should be. Help students to learn to read and predict the missing words using context clues. Challenge students to guess and spell the missing words by reading the surrounding text. Tell them that this is a simple strategy for understanding unfamiliar words.

Name _____ Date _____

Book Re-cover-ing

Title: _____

Author: _____

Illustrator: _____

Favorite Passage or Part:

_____

_____

_____

_____

_____

_____

83 Spell It Out!

Give students plenty of practice blending *consonant-consonant-vowel-consonant-consonant* (ccvcc) sounds into words. Provide each student with a marker and a small whiteboard or writing tablet. Tell students to listen to the five letter sounds (phonemes) you say. Have them say what word you made. Encourage students to write the letters they hear on their boards to help them spell the word. For example, say to students: "Listen to these sounds—/b/ /l/ /e/ /n/ /d/. What sounds did you hear? What word did I make?" Prompt them to raise their hands when they think they know the word. Print the five letters on chart paper, and have students copy the letters on their boards. Have them recite the sounds separately to connect sounds to letters and then blend the sounds into the whole word. Repeat this activity several times by using different ccvcc letter combinations to say and spell words. This is a great strategy for reinforcing the connection between spoken words and words in print.

84 Retelling with Setting Maps

Help children retell familiar stories by making setting maps! Read aloud a folktale such as *The Three Little Pigs.* Then let children work in small cooperative groups to draw a map of the setting. Tell children to retell the story in their groups and list places they want to include on their maps. They can go through the book or story and identify all the different settings in which story events take place. Give each group large pieces of butcher paper on which to draw their maps. Encourage students to draw houses and buildings, as well as trees, bushes, flowers, and other nature items, to cut out and glue on their maps. Instruct students how to make a compass rose and key for their maps.

Next, read an alternative version of the famous folktale called *The True Story of the Three Little Pigs* by Jon Scieszka. Instruct students to draw a map for this version of the same story and compare it to their original map. Have them identify all the story elements that are alike and different. Include discussion on the narrator's point of view and each story's resolution. Invite each group to use its map as a guide to write a retelling of the stories and then present to the class. Have them point out the similarities and differences.

85 Alphabetical Order

Help students learn and apply their knowledge of alphabetical order using your classroom library. Buy several different colors of duct tape. Cut a small strip of colored tape for each book that has a title beginning with the letter *A*. Print the letter *A* on the strips and attach one to the binding of each book. Choose a different color tape for books that have titles beginning with the letter *B*, and so on. Explain to students that titles starting with the word *The* or *A* will be alphabetized by the first letter of the second word. Discuss the need for this rule and give examples. For example, *The Cat in the Hat* would be filed under *C*, not *T*.

Explain to children that you need their help keeping the books on the shelves in alphabetical order. Show them where the alphabet strip is located for each book and how to arrange the letters according to the alphabet. By alternating different colors for the letters, children will have color as well as letter clues to help them correctly arrange the books.

Practice alphabetizing often by scrambling several books and encouraging students to find and correct your errors. To challenge them further, try rearranging books that have the same color coding, but different letters. Also arrange books for each letter into sections such as *Ai–Al, Am–Ar, As–Aw* to give students the opportunity to alphabetize to the second and third letters of words.

86 Cross-Curricular Sorting Words

Have students learn to identify and sort words into categories. Make sorting kits using word cards and small paper bags. First, think of cross-curricular categories in which to sort things, such as *Vertebrates, Nouns, State Capitals,* and *Money*. On tagboard cards, print the names of items belonging in each category. For example: *Vertebrates—eagle, goldfish, rattlesnake, frog, horse; Money—dollar, penny, nickel, dime, quarter;* and so on. Then place two to three categories of word cards in each bag. Prepare several category bags, one for each student, if possible. Number the bags. Let students choose their bags and sort the words into categories. For extra fun, include pictures as well, so children can match pictures and words in each category. Invite them to switch bags with classmates and sort the new words.

Provide an extra challenge by including words from a recent vocabulary study. Encourage students to sort words into categories such as *measurements, shapes,* and so on.

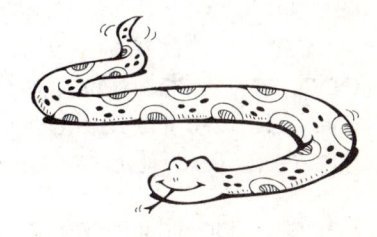

87 What Do You See?

Good readers visualize while they are reading. They may visualize the setting of the story or the expression on a character's face. Get students to visualize text by using one of the techniques listed below.

- Ask questions that lead students to mental pictures
- Think aloud
- Model visualization
- Draw, paint, or sculpt images, scenes, or characters
- Write descriptions of what they see in their imaginations
- Act out what they see happening
- Doodling or sketching
- Hold group discussions
- Use visual aides

When students create mental images about a scene or character, they are more likely to identify with the character or remember the details of the setting. Use a variety of techniques to get students to visualize while reading. Keep them practicing until it becomes second nature, and they do it without even thinking!

88 "You Say Tomato..."

Ask students to identify expressions or sayings in the context of their reading. Provide several examples of what you want students to look for. They can be regional expressions from different parts of the country, or cultural expressions from different countries or cultures. For example, note these old Southern expressions: *Cut the tail off a dog* means "Make a long story short," and *The same dog bit me* means "I feel the same way about it."

Choose material for students to read that may include some expressions and sayings. Invite students to read the text silently. After everyone has finished reading, ask, "Can anyone find an example of a regional or cultural saying?" For example, the terms *y'all* and *I'm fixin' to . . .* are typically used in the South. Talk about how the sayings or expressions reflect the region or culture from which they derive. Invite students to guess why the author included that expression in the text. Ask, "Do these kinds of expressions add to the authenticity of the text?"

Encourage students to share expressions that are used in their families or with friends. Ask them to investigate these sayings to find out from where they originated and who uses them most.

© McGraw-Hill Children's Publishing

0-7424-2698-X *Every Teacher Is a Reading Teacher: 101 Ways to Incorporate Reading into Your Classroom*

89 Lost Art of Letter Writing

Discover the lost art of letter writing! Read several books which include characters communicating through letter writing. Spend time examining each one's style and voice. As a group, practice writing a letter to one of the characters, focusing on format and structure. Reread and refer to the books for examples.

Books with Letters
Dear Annie by Judith Caseley
The Jolly Postman by Allan Ahlberg
Messages in the Mailbox: How to Write a Letter by Loreen Leedy
With Love, Little Red Hen by Alma Flor Ada
Yours Truly, Goldilocks by Alma Flor Ada

Discuss the occasions when writing a personal letter is important. Guide the conversation toward writing thank-you letters. Ask students to think of people in their school community who help them every day. Write a list of school workers on the board to inspire the thinking process, such as *cafeteria worker, librarian, secretary, principal, teacher, custodian, teacher's aide*. Invite volunteers to share some of their special memories and experiences.

Then tell students they will be writing thank-you notes to one of these special people. Show sample thank-you notes and cards to students, and point out features such as the greeting, message, and signature.

First, have students write thank-you notes on scrap paper. Tell them to use the "Letter Writing Checklist" on page 112 to revise their writing. Point out that they will be answering questions about their writing. Discuss what the questions mean, and provide examples on the board. Tell students that these questions give them information that will make their writing better. Guide them to understand that reading and writing go hand in hand. As students use the checklist repeatedly with various writing assignments, they will begin to read and respond to the questions on their own!

For an extra challenge, invite partners to fill out a "Letter Writing Checklist" for a partner's work or some of the sample thank-you notes and cards you brought to class. They can also practice by applying the questions to previous writing assignments.

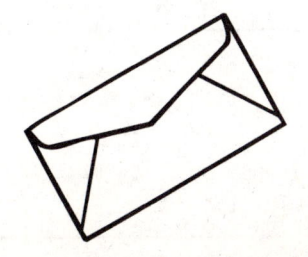

Name _____ Date _____

Letter Writing Checklist

1. Answer each question about your writing. Mark an **X** in the **Yes** or **No** column.

Yes	No	
❏	❏	Are there any missing words?
❏	❏	Are there any extra words?
❏	❏	Do all sentences make sense? Are they complete?
❏	❏	Do all sentences begin with a capital letter?
❏	❏	Are all the correct words capitalized?
❏	❏	Do all sentences end with a punctuation mark? (**.** or **!** or **?**)
❏	❏	Are any words misspelled?
❏	❏	Are there good describing words?

2. How can you make the writing better? Be specific!

_____
_____
_____
_____
_____
_____
_____

© McGraw-Hill Children's Publishing

0-7424-2698-X *Every Teacher Is a Reading Teacher: 101 Ways to Incorporate Reading into Your Classroom*

90 A Report on Prediction

Help students practice making predictions about text by writing a "Prediction Report." Make a copy of the "Prediction Report" form on page 114 for each student. Use a picture book as a sample and demonstrate how to complete the form on an overhead transparency. Then have students take the form with them to the library when selecting their own books.

Encourage students to select a fiction book. For this activity, a chapter book works best, but the activity can be slightly modified to incorporate other books.

Instructions for "Prediction Report":

1. Select a book. Write the title, author, and illustrator's names on the book report form.

2. Read the summary on the back of the book and the first page of text. Write a short statement predicting what you think the book will be about.

3. Read the first two chapters of the book or the first two or three pages of a picture book. Then make another prediction about what you think will happen. Is this book different than you thought it would be?

4. Continue reading the book, but do not read the last chapter. Predict what you think will happen at the end of the book. Give reasons from the text to support your prediction.

5. Finally, finish the book and adjust your predictions.

6. Think about whether or not you would recommend this book to a friend. Explain your reasons.

Some helpful hints:

- It is important to demonstrate how to complete the form before students attempt it on their own.

- Steps 1 and 2 can be completed while in the library if time allows.

- Since this activity takes more than one day to complete, suggest students place the form in a safe place. For example, tell them to clip it into their reading journals.

- Require students to make predictions while they are reading. Avoid having students reading ahead and then going back to fill in the form.

- Some students may be uncomfortable making predictions. Explain how predictions are never wrong but simply an expression of one's opinion about the text. However, challenge students to provide reasons to support their predictions.

Name _____ Date _____

Prediction Report

Title: _____

Author: _____

Illustrator: _____

1. Read the summary and the first page of the book. What do you think this book is going to be about?

   _____

   _____

2. Read the first two chapters of the book. What do you think will happen next in this story? Is this book what you thought it was going to be?

   _____

   _____

3. Before you read the last chapter of the book, predict the ending. What do you think is going to happen at the end? Give examples from the story to tell why you think this will happen.

   _____

   _____

4. Read the rest of the book. Did the ending match your prediction? Did the ending surprise you? Was it what you expected? Why or why not?

   _____

   _____

5. Would you recommend this book to a friend? Why or why not?

   _____

   _____

91 Power of Persuasion

Use literature as a springboard for writing a persuasive essay. Find an example in literature of a problem or important issue. Some examples include cheating in school, wearing a helmet while riding a bicycle, lying to parents or friends, and sharing with others. The problem might be explicitly stated, or students may build upon what they discover in the text. The issue may be a current serious issue in our world or a dilemma common to many young people at home or at school.

Example 1: While reading the book *Chocolate Fever* by Robert Kimmel Smith, point out Henry's dilemma. He is allowed to eat chocolate as much as he wants and whenever he wants. Posing as Henry's doctor, write a letter to Henry persuading him to eat chocolate only in moderation, and explain the benefits of eating well-balanced meals.

Example 2: Take an issue implied in the text and build a persuasive argument about a real-life problem. When Henry starts to grow brown spots all over his body, no one knows what they are, and people start to treat him differently. Write a persuasive essay about the effects of judging others before you have all the facts.

Review the elements of persuasive writing with students before they begin their essays. A persuasive composition should employ some of the following techniques listed below to convince the reader.

- Support an argument with reasons
- Appeal to emotions
- Use pro and con statements
- Use facts, statistics, examples, or quotes
- Address the reader's concerns and feelings
- Use powerful images

92 Getting Acquainted

Before reading a new chapter book or textbook, spend time getting acquainted with the book. Demonstrate for students how to get information from the title, copyright, and dedication pages. Explore the table of contents, the glossary, and any indices. Skim through the chapters looking at chapter titles, guide words, captions, illustrations, and diagrams. Note any special highlighted words or phrases.

Think and ask questions aloud as you look at each page, and model for students how you are wondering about the book and its contents. Make predictions and use previous knowledge to link concepts together. Occasionally assign this kind of activity for homework. Tell students that they shouldn't actually read the chapter, and they are just getting acquainted with their books the night before you begin a new unit.

93 Read, Watch, Compare

Read the classics together! As a whole class or in small groups, read a children's classic together. Examine the story elements and help students make connections to their own lives. When everyone has finished the book, find a movie rendition of the same story. Watch it together and make a comparison. Refer to the book for similarities and differences. Be specific and provide several examples. If parts of the book were edited for the movie, talk about possible reasons for that decision. Ask, "Did the movie follow the book's plot?" "Was the movie easier to follow because you were familiar with the characters and the background information?" "Which version did you prefer, and why?" "How would you change the movie if you could?"

Classic Books
Eloise: The Ultimate Edition by Kay Thompson
How the Grinch Stole Christmas! by Dr. Seuss
Jumanji by Chris Van Allsburg
Madeline by Ludwig Bemelmans
The Magic School Bus Series by Joanna Cole

94 Jumping Genres

Read or tell a common childhood story or fable, such as *The Three Little Pigs* or *The Boy Who Cried Wolf*. Ask students to adapt the story into a different literary form or genre.

Brainstorm with students the features of various literary genres. Invite volunteers to supply a list of genres with which they are familiar. For example, fiction, nonfiction, drama, poetry, folktale, fairy tale, mystery. Ask for details that describe the characteristics of each genre. Write responses on the board or chart paper, and leave it in view for student reference.

Then arrange students in small groups, and assign each group one type or genre of literature. Give each group a different story from their assigned genre. If possible, assign a different genre to each group. Use stories with which students are familiar, such as the Aesop's fable *The Fox and the Grapes*, the folktale *Little Red Riding Hood*, or the fairy tale *Rumpelstiltskin*. Instruct each group to create its own version of the assigned story using a different genre. For example, if the group is assigned the fable *The Fox and the Grapes*, have them rewrite the fable as a fairy tale or poem! Remind students to refer to the brainstorming list to note the characteristics of the genre. Other ideas for rewrites include creating a script for a play or dramatic reading, fictional picture book, or research report about a fact related to the story, such as the habitat of foxes.

Invite groups to present their work to the class. They can perform a play, read a poem, or discuss their research. After all groups have had a chance to share, ask students to respond to the question: "How did the story change with each literary form?" Ask students to respond in their journals.

95 "Personally, I think..."

Students better comprehend and engage with text when they feel personally connected to it. Experienced readers will find connections without even trying if something in the story is familiar or has personal meaning to them. You can help students hone their comprehension skills and find personal connections with text by using the "Personal Connections Map" on page 119.

The "Personal Connections Map" can be used before, during, or after reading. To use the map before reading, provide students with an engaging passage from the text that will stimulate thinking or generate interest. During reading, ask students to select a passage that has immediate personal meaning. After reading, have students select the passage that best captured their attention and is particularly memorable.

No matter in what stage of the reading it is used, the process remains the same. Begin by writing a passage in the left box on the map. The passage can be a quote from the text or a paraphrase. For easy reference, include the location of the passage in the text, such as page and paragraph number in the book, line number in the poem, page and paragraph number in the article. Students will then make the connection and record personal responses in the right box. Write the prompts below on chart paper and post them in students' view.

- I know about this because . . .
- This happened to me when . . .
- I feel/felt like this when . . .
- I had a similar experience when . . .
- I know how that feels because . . .
- I already know . . .
- This reminds me of . . .

Encourage students to share their insights with a partner, in a literature circle, or with the entire class. However, be aware of students' personal privacy, and make sure that sensitive material is shared voluntarily. Invite students to share how these personal connections made the text more meaningful to them.

Name _____ Date _____

Personal Connections Map

Copy or summarize a passage from the text. Include the title, page number, and paragraph number from the book or article. Write your personal response next to the passage.

Title:_____

Page # _____ **Paragraph #** _____
Describe the Passage:
_____
_____
_____
_____

Page # _____ **Paragraph #** _____
Describe the Passage:
_____
_____
_____
_____

Page # _____ **Paragraph #** _____
Describe the Passage:
_____
_____
_____
_____

Page # _____ **Paragraph #** _____
Describe the Passage:
_____
_____
_____
_____

Page # _____ **Paragraph #** _____
Describe the Passage:
_____
_____
_____
_____

Page # _____ **Paragraph #** _____
Describe the Passage:
_____
_____
_____
_____

96 "Called, Cried, Cackled"

Most students are learning about dialogue and their skills for writing dialogue are just emerging. The word *said* is usually repeated endlessly and applied to every situation. Encourage students to expand their vocabulary to include more expressive and specific words when writing dialogue.

Photocopy a page from a book with lots of dialogue. Ask students to highlight the words that indicate a person is speaking, and then list these words on a sheet of paper. Have them work in small groups to brainstorm additional words. Give each group a thesaurus so they can search for more alternatives or synonyms. Groups should list at least three alternatives for each word. Encourage students to keep the list handy when writing dialogue and add to it as they encounter new words.

As an extension, challenge students to rewrite the page, replacing the dialogue words, such as *said* and *asked*, with more interesting words from their lists. When finished ask, "Does this make the reading more interesting and exciting?"

Sample Word List:
- added
- answered
- asked
- bellowed
- called
- cried
- expressed
- hissed
- laughed
- giggled
- groaned
- mumbled
- murmured
- pleaded
- queried
- questioned
- replied
- screamed
- screeched
- shouted
- shrieked
- sighed
- whimpered
- whined
- whispered
- yelled

97 Vocabulary Builders

Prior to reading a story, have students skim through the text to search for unfamiliar words. Make a list on chart paper of any unfamiliar words. Working in pairs, have students use a dictionary or thesaurus to find and write definitions or synonyms for every unrecognized word. Tell them to keep a running list of new words and their meanings in their reading journals. Suggest that they keep their journals nearby while reading the story for quick reference.

After reading the story for comprehension, review the word list on the chart. Ask students to give examples from the story that use each word. Invite volunteers to use the words in new sentences, and apply their understanding outside the context of the reading. Continue to add to the word list, and review the words often. Challenge students to look for these words in other readings and in their surrounding environment.

98 Fun with Fluency

Invite students to practice fluency with tongue twisters and poems! Some of the best poetry takes practice in reading aloud. Demonstrate how to read poetry by using expression and emphasizing the beat or rhythm. Explain to students that to get the rhythm down, poems need to be read several times. Model for students by snapping your fingers or tapping your toes on emphasis words in several examples. Read each example a few times to show how rereading makes the poem smoother, more familiar, and even lyrical.

Distribute a wide variety of poems to students. Have them work in pairs to practice reading poems together. Instruct them to focus on the musical beat of the lines and understanding every word. Ask pairs to take turns standing up and reading their poems together. Then ask individual volunteers to read aloud for the whole group.

Age-appropriate Poetry
Falling Up by Shel Silverstein
If I Were in Charge of the World and Other Worries: Poems for Children and Their Parents by Judith Viorst
A Light in the Attic by Shel Silverstein
The New Kid on the Block by Jack Prelutsky
Oh, the Thinks You Can Think! by Dr. Seuss
The Random House Book of Poetry for Children selected by Jack Prelutsky
The Stinky Cheese Man and Other Fairly Stupid Tales by Jon Scieszka
Where the Sidewalk Ends by Shel Silverstein

PHYSICAL EDUCATION, ART, AND MUSIC

Physical Education

99 All About Sports

Invite students to choose and read books about sports or favorite athletes. Personal selection of titles is important for this activity. Allowing students to choose their own books gives them a sense of ownership and will help sustain interest in the text. First, have students skim through the book, looking at photos, illustrations, headings, and featured words and phrases. Ask them to predict what they think the book might be about.

After reading their books, ask students to research something in the text. For example, if a student reads a biography of Wayne Gretzky, he can research the history of Lord Stanley's Cup. If a student reads a book about soccer rules, she can research the history of soccer. If a student reads a book about bicycle racing, he can research the life of Lance Armstrong. Encourage students to choose a narrow aspect of something mentioned in the book and use it as a springboard for further research.

Give students the following directions for research:

1. Read the book you have chosen.
2. Write the title, author and illustrator's names, and a summary of the story.
3. Select a person, thing, or event from the book that you would like to investigate and learn more about.
4. Conduct research about the person, thing, or event. Use a variety of resources, including books, magazines, encyclopedias, and Internet resources. Take notes on your research.
5. Highlight the five most important facts you want to share about your chosen person, thing, or event.
6. Describe the connection between the book and your research. What else did you learn about this sport or athlete?
7. Share your work with the class. Give an oral presentation to discuss what you learned.

Suggested Titles for Physical Education

The age ranges and levels of these books vary. Use them according to students' needs, interests, and abilities.

Baseball Saved Us by Ken Mochizuki
A Day in the Life of a Coach by Mary Bowman-Kruhm and Claudine G. Wirths
Froggy Plays Soccer by Jonathan London
Honus and Me: A Baseball Card Adventure by Dan Gutman
Hooray for the Dandelion Warriors! by Bill Cosby
Hooray for Snail! by John Stadler
In the Year of the Boar and Jackie Robinson by Bette Bao Lord
Lance Armstrong: The Race of His Life by Kristin Armstrong
Lives of the Athletes: Thrills, Spills (and What the Neighbors Thought) by Kathleen Krull
NBA Action from A to Z by Brendan Hanrahan
Play Ball, Amelia Bedelia by Peggy Parish
Princess Fidgety Feet by Pat Posner
Salt in His Shoes by Deloris Jordan and Roslyn M. Jordan
Satchel Paige by Lesa Cline-Ransome
Seabiscuit vs War Admiral: The Greatest Horse Race in History by Kat Shehata
Soccer Duel by Matt Christopher (or any other books by Matt Christopher)
S.O.R. Losers by Avi
Sports: Hall of Fame by Morgan Hughes
Sports in Action Series
Teammates by Peter Golenbock
Wilma Unlimited: How Wilma Rudolph Became the World's Fastest Woman by Kathleen Krull
Z is for Zamboni: A Hockey Alphabet by Matt Napier

Art

100 Presenting Art

Ask students to choose a fiction or nonfiction book related to art. The book might be about an art museum, a biography of a famous artist, or an instructional book about crafting or painting. Whatever the subject matter, remind students to choose a book related to art or an art theme. Provide a suggested reading list, or encourage students to search the library. Once students have made a selection, allow adequate time for them to complete the reading.

After reading their books, have students deliver an oral presentation. Ask students to present all of the components listed below.

- Title, author, illustrator
- Summary
- Type of art described in book (provide examples)
- Personal opinion of the book
- Examples to support your opinion
- Historical time period and perspective of book
- Any art projects or posters of art

Encourage students to show at least one sample of the type of art featured in the book. Students may bring a picture of a painting or sculpture, or paint their own picture imitating the artist's technique! If a student reads an instructional book, invite him or her to complete an art project and share it with the class. Encourage students to explore and use their creativity!

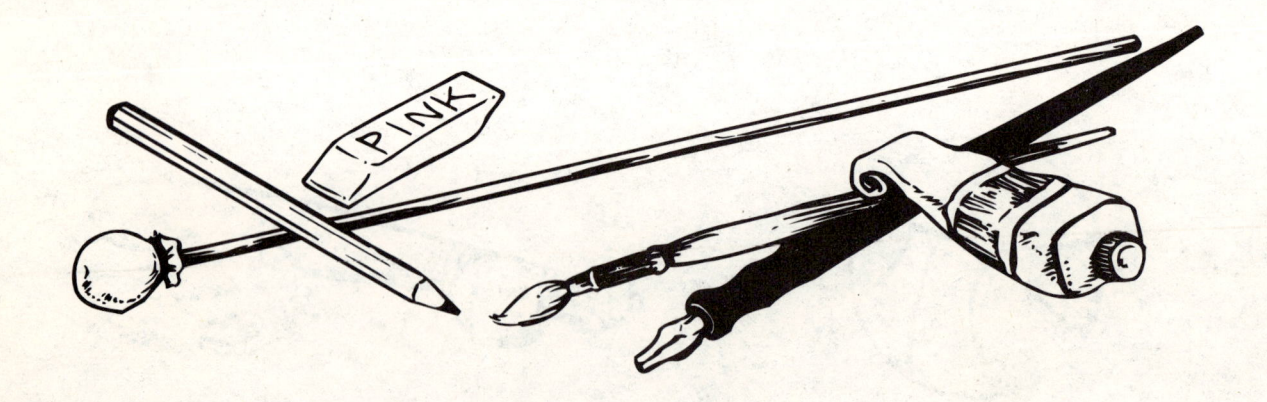

Suggested Titles for Art

The age ranges and levels of these books vary. Use them according to students' needs, interests, and abilities.

All About You by Catherine Anholt
Art Activity Pack Series by Mila Boutan
Art Attack: A Brief Cultural History of the Avant-Garde by Marc Aronson
Art for Children Series by Baumbusch
Celebrate America in Poetry and Art edited by Nora Panzer
Celebrating America: A Collection of Poems and Images of the American Spirit compiled by Laura Whipple
A Child's Book of Art: Discover Great Paintings by Lucy Micklethwait
Chrysanthemum by Kevin Henkes
Cleversticks by Bernard Ashley
A Drawing in the Sand: A Story of African American Art by Jerry Butler
From Pictures to Words: A Book About Making a Book by Janet Stevens
From the Mixed-up Files of Mrs. Basil E. Frankweiler by E. L. Konigsburg
Getting to Know the World's Greatest Artists Series by Mike Venezia
Harry and Willy and Carrothead by Judith Caseley
History of Art for Young People by H. W. Janson and Anthony F. Janson
I Like Me! by Nancy Carlson
Leonardo and the Flying Boy: A Story About Leonardo Da Vinci by Laurence Anholt
Linnea in Monet's Garden by Cristina Bjork
Marianthe's Story: Painted Words, Spoken Memories by Aliki
Off the Wall Museum Guides for Kids Series by Ruthie Knapp and Janice Lehmberg
Understanding Modern Art by Monica Bohm-Duchen, et al.
Weaving a California Tradition: A Native American Basketmaker by Linda Yamane
What Do Illustrators Do? by Eileen Christelow
What Makes Cassatt a Cassatt? by Richard Muhlberger and The Metropolitan Museum of Art
When Pigasso Met Mootisse by Nina Laden

Music

101 Magical Music

Introduce students to reading about music by focusing on the familiar concept of marching bands and orchestras! Ask questions such as: "Has anyone ever seen a marching band or been to a concert?" "What kinds of instruments did you see and hear?" "What are your favorite instruments?" List some of these instruments on the board, such as *trumpet, flute, drums, tuba, clarinet, piccolo, oboe, violin, cello, viola, bass, saxophone*. Describe any instruments with which students are not familiar, and invite them to make the sounds of the instruments.

Continue your discussion by explaining that music is a vast industry that employs thousands of people behind the scenes, like music producers and promoters, as well as onstage, like musicians and singers. Ask each student to complete a short research project about a career in the music industry. They can research their favorite singers or groups, a famous composer, or an orchestra musician. Suggest some of additional careers in music, such as: producer, recording engineer, stage manager, songwriter, music publicist, record promoter, and artist rep.

To conduct their research, invite students to work in small groups. They can use online resources, books, magazines, personal interviews, biographies, and more. Encourage students to find out the skills required for the job, the level of education needed, and the typical work required of a person in that profession. For example, they may want to ask find out about the typical day of an orchestra musician or record producer.

While reading, have students note specific terms and language associated with their chosen career. Encourage them to feature these words in their final presentations. Groups can play music during their presentation, bring in or show a picture of a featured instrument, or invite a special guest to discuss his or her job. You may want to employ the help of adult volunteers or aides to help groups with their presentations.

Suggested Titles for Music

The age ranges and levels of these books vary. Use them according to students' needs, interests, and abilities.

Bat Boy and His Violin by Gavin Curtis
Beethoven Lives Upstairs by Barbara Nichol
Dance Me a Story: Twelve Tales from the Classic Ballets by Jane Rosenberg
Ella Fitzgerald: The Tale of a Vocal Virtuosa by Andrea Davis Pinkney
Getting to Know the World's Greatest Composers Series by Mike Venezia
Great Composers Series
Hip Cat by Jonathan London
I Like the Music by Leah Komaiko
Jazz Fly by Matthew Gollub
Lentil by Robert McCloskey
Meet the Orchestra by Ann Hayes
Parade by Donald Crews
Play to the Angel by Maurine F. Dahlberg
Sing Me a Story: The Metropolitan Opera's Book of Opera Stories for Children by Jane Rosenberg
The Story of the Incredible Orchestra: An Introduction to Musical Instruments and the Symphony Orchestra by Bruce Koscielniak
Tchaikovsky Discovers America by Esther Kalman
When Marian Sang: The True Recital of Marian Anderson by Pam Munoz Ryan
The World of Composers Series: Bach, Beethoven, Chopin, Handel, Mozart, Tchaikovsky, Verdi, Wagner by Greta Cencetti
Yolanda's Genius by Carol Fenner
Zin! Zin! Zin! A Violin by Lloyd Moss

Congratulations
Reading Superstar!

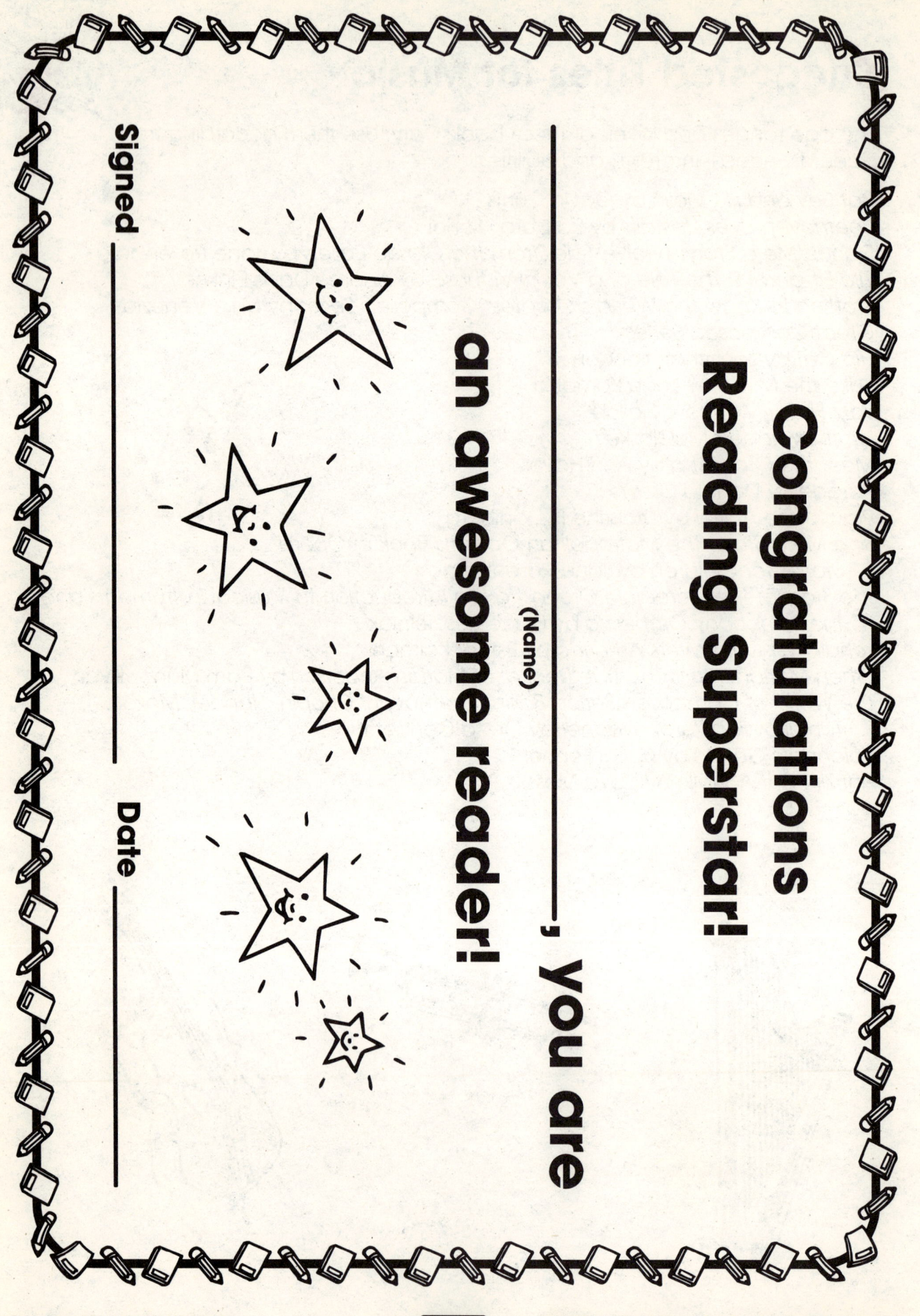

_____
(Name)

, you are

an awesome reader!

Signed _____

Date _____

© McGraw-Hill Children's Publishing

0-7424-2698-X *Every Teacher Is a Reading Teacher:*
101 Ways to Incorporate Reading into Your Classroom